WORLD Without fISH

MARK KURLANSKY

WORLD

Without fish

HOW COULD
WE LET THIS
HAPPEN?

WORKMAN PUBLISHING · NEW YORK

Library of Congress Cataloging-in-Publication Data is available.

ISBN: 978-0-7611-8500-0

Design by Raquel Jaramillo

Photo/art credits: xii, Courtesy of Library of Congress; xviii, Courtesy of U.S. National
Ocean and Atmospheric Administration; xxii, Dorling Kindersley/Getty Images; xxiii,
© Toru Yamanaka/AFP/Getty Images; 3 (top), Courtesy of U.S. National Ocean and
Atmospheric Administration; 3 (right), © HelleM/Shutterstock; 5, © D. Morley Read/
Shutterstock; 9, © Roblind/Shutterstock; 10, © Rich Lindie/Shutterstock; 11, © Jeff Foott/
Getty Images; 14, © Yomiuri Shimbun/AFP/Getty Images; 16, © Dorling Kindersley/Getty
Images; 25, © Hulton Archive/Getty Images; 26, ©Kovaleska/Shutterstock; 29, Various/
Shutterstock; 31, ILN Print Library; 46, © WILDLIFE GmbH/Alamy; 54, Courtesy of
Rijksmuseum, Amsterdam; 56, Courtesy of Wikipedia Commons; 58, Prints-4-All;
67, © Jennifer Pavelski/Shutterstock; 69, Courtesy of Wikipedia Commons; 83, © Stacy
Gold/National Geographic/Getty Images; 90, Courtesy of Wikipedia Commons; 95, © Jeff
Rotman/Getty Images; 104, Dorling Kindersley/Getty Images; 111, © Laura Stone/Shut-
terstock; 120, © Telnov Oleg/Shutterstock; 124, © Danny E. Hooks/Shutterstock; 130,
© Astrid van der Eerden/Shutterstock; 148, © Anna Segeren/Shutterstock; 152, Courtesy
of U.S. Federal Government; 154, Courtesy of Marine Stewardship Council; 155, 177,
Courtesy of Monterey Bay Aquarium

This label verifies that the forest products used in
the manufacturing of this book have been responsibly
harvested from verified sources.

Workman Publishing Company, Inc.
225 Varick Street
New York, NY 10014-4381
workman.com

Printed in the United States of America
First paperback printing November 2014

10 9 8

TO MARIAN AND TALIA
AND OUR LIFE BY THE SEA

CONTENTS

BEING A BRIEF OUTLINE OF THE PROBLEM

A large stock of individuals of the same species, relative to the number of its enemies, is absolutely necessary for its preservation.
—Charles Darwin, ON THE ORIGIN OF SPECIES

MOST STORIES ABOUT THE DESTRUCTION OF THE PLANET INVOLVE A VILLAIN WITH AN EVIL PLOT.

BUT THIS IS THE STORY OF HOW THE EARTH COULD BE DESTROYED

BY WELL-MEANING PEOPLE WHO FAIL TO SOLVE A PROBLEM SIMPLY BECAUSE THEIR CALCULATIONS ARE WRONG.

MOST OF THE FISH WE COMMONLY EAT, MOST OF THE FISH WE KNOW, COULD BE GONE IN THE NEXT FIFTY YEARS.

THIS INCLUDES SALMON, TUNA, COD, SWORDFISH, and anchovies. If this happens, many other fish that depend on these fish will also be in trouble. So will seabirds that eat fish, such as seagulls and cormorants. So will mammals that eat fish, such as whales, porpoises, and seals. And insects that depend on seabirds, such as beetles and lizards. And mammals that depend on beetles and lizards. Slowly—or maybe not so slowly—in less time than the several billion years it took to create it—life on planet Earth could completely unravel.

People who are in school today are lucky to have been born at a special moment in history. The Industrial Revolution, beginning in the mid-eighteenth century and continuing for the next 120 years shifted production from handcrafts to machine-made factory goods and in so doing completely changed the relationship of people to nature, the relationship of people to each other, politics, art, and architecture—the look and thought of the world. In the next fifty years, much of your working life, there will be as much change in less than half the time. The future of the world, perhaps even

THE SURVIVAL OF THE PLANET, WILL DEPEND ON HOW WELL THESE CHANGES ARE HANDLED. AND SO YOU HAVE MORE OPPORTUNITIES AND MORE RESPONSIBILITIES THAN ANY OTHER GENERATION IN HISTORY.

CHARLES DARWIN
(February 12, 1809–
April 19 1882)
Darwin was born, coincidentally, on the same day as Abraham Lincoln, another great thinker of his age.

ONE OF THE GREAT THINKERS of the Industrial Revolution was an Englishman named Charles Darwin. In 1859, he had published one of the most important books ever written: *On the Origin of Species by Means of Natural Selection, or the Preservation of Favoured Races in the Struggle for Life*, more commonly known by its shortened title: *On the Origin of Species*.

In his book, Darwin explained the order

of nature as a system in which all the many various plant and animal species struggle for survival. He did not see nature as particularly nice or kind, but as a cruel system in which species attempted to kill and dominate other species in order to secure the survival of their own kind. He wrote, "We do not see, or we forget, that the birds which are idly singing round us, mostly live on insects or seeds, and are thus constantly destroying life."

Plants and animals are organized into groups with seven major levels or categories: KINGDOM, PHYLUM, CLASS, ORDER, FAMILY, GENUS (PLURAL: GENERA), SPECIES.

A good way to remember the seven major categories of animal and plant classification is with this sentence: "Kangaroos play cellos, orangutans fiddle, gorillas sing."

A codfish and a human belong to the same kingdom, which is animals. They also belong to the same phylum, which is vertebrates (animals with spines). But after that, they break off into completely different classes—cod are fish and humans are mammals. More specifically, humans are vertebrates of the class known as mammals in the order known as primates, which we share with monkeys and lemurs. We belong to the family Hominidae, which we share with apes and chimpanzees. Within that family, we are of the genus *Homo*, which are Hominidae that walk standing up on two feet. (Several other *Homo* genera have all died off and we are the only surviving species of this family: *Homo sapiens*.) Cod, on the other hand, are fish—specifically fish with jaws—that belong to a family called Gadidae. This fish family is fairly evolved, has elaborate fins, and lives in the bottom part of the ocean. They hunt voraciously the species living directly over and beneath them, and have white flesh greatly favored by *Homo sapiens*.

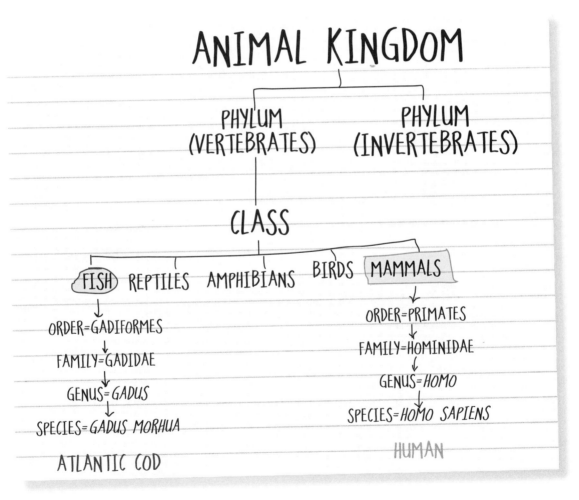

Darwin wrote of how all species struggle for the survival of their own group. So it is not surprising that we humans have the greatest affection for organisms that are biologically close to us. Killing our own species is the worst thing we can do. Killing close relatives to our species, like monkeys, though it occurs, is revolting to most of us. We tend to care more about our own class—mammals, such as whales and seals and polar bears—than we do about fish. Is that because they are in a different class? Is that why people tend to have less sympathy for animals that are not in our phylum, like insects? Ultimately, a vegetarian is a human who rejects killing living things from his own kingdom—animals—but accepts killing from the other kingdom—plants.

DARWIN'S GREAT CONTRIBUTION WAS TO understand that in the struggle for survival, nature puts out variations: the species that successfully adapt through the use of variations survive, and the others become extinct. Our family, Hominidae, was a very successful family because it developed numerous variations that went on to be successful genera and developed various species. The genus *Homo* produced one highly successful species that dominated while the other *Homo* genera became extinct.

Darwin's ideas were extremely controversial in 1859. Some people were upset that he did not see nature as kind. Others thought his vision of how humans evolved conflicted with what was written in the Bible. They did not like the idea that he accorded no special mystery to the creation of man, that it was just another animal created by chance experimentation in nature. Nor did they want to accept the idea that natural experimentation led to the development of the species and that they did not each appear in a separate act of creation. There are people who are still angry about Darwin because they believe his theories conflict with the Bible. But most people, whether they believe in the Bible or not, think that Darwin's explanation of natural order makes sense. For a century and a half now, scientists have been observing natural occurrences and have found that they follow the theories of Darwin.

As the millions of other species of plants and animals struggled for survival, circumstances were constantly changing. Species moved into and out of areas, there were changes in weather, some species were eliminated and others became extremely abundant. Each shift, sometimes as minuscule as a shift in the wind, day by day—even hour by hour—changed the order of nature. These shifts continue to happen, so slightly that we don't even notice. But things are changing and, over time, these changes can be enormous.

As circumstances change, there are variations in species—sometimes a change in color, or a tendency to hunt in a certain way. These changes can be thought of as experiments. Some fail and disappear and some succeed and become a completely different species. It is out of this process, known as evolution, that monkeys eventually developed into human beings.

In understanding what is happening in the oceans today, it is essential to understand the Darwinian order of life. Though Darwin wrote only a little about the sea, marine life is linked in the same system as all life on Earth.

ALL LIFE ON EARTH IS INTERCONNECTED, AND ALTERED CIRCUMSTANCES WILL CHANGE THE ORDER OF LIFE AT SEA, WHICH WILL ALSO CHANGE LIFE ON LAND. AND ALL OF THIS CAN AND WILL HAVE AN ENORMOUS IMPACT ON OUR LIVES.

It is important to understand that there are *not* two worlds: the world of humans and a separate world of plants and animals. There isn't a "natural world" and a "man-made world." We all live on the same planet and live in the same natural order. What plants and animals do alters human life, and what humans do alters plant and animal life. Even the smallest changes can have unforseen results that are extremely difficult to change back.

DARWIN NOTED THAT FOR A SPECIES to survive it must have large numbers because it has enemies that kill its kind. What that means is that not every individual member of the species must die in order for the entire species to die off. It only has to lose a large enough percentage of its kind to have little chance of survival. In fishing, a distinction is made between a fish species that is biologically extinct and one that is commercially extinct. Only very rarely do we find the biological extinction of a fish, where a fish species has not one single living specimen. But commercial extinction, which is when there are so few of a particular kind of fish that it is no longer profitable to fish for them is increasingly common. For instance, the North American Atlantic salmon is commercially extinct because it has only hundreds rather than hundreds of thousands of surviving fish. It is unknown whether the few survivors will ever be able to reproduce enough to once again be the flourishing stock that they used to be. If that is the case, if the number is so low that the species is no longer plentiful enough for survival, it may become biologically extinct and completely disappear from the ocean.

NORTH ATLANTIC SALMON
(*Salmo salar*)
This species, unlike the Alaska Wild Salmon, is on the brink of commercial extinction.

IN SCIENCE, IT IS KNOWN THAT LIFE depends on a large variety. This is known as biodiversity. The fewer species—the less bio-diversity—the harder it will be for the re-maining species to survive. And that includes us, human beings. Remember, we are the only surviving species of our genus, *Homo*.

Though the term *biodiversity* was first coined by biologists in 1986—and came into common usage at a meeting of biologists in 1988—the concept was writ-ten about by Darwin in *On the Origin of Species*. He stated it simply: "The greatest amount of life can be supported by great diversification."

We have named a million species in the world. We know of another 800,000 that we have not yet given names. Scientists guess that there are at least ten million species in the world, though there may be even more. This means that

MOST SPECIES HAVE YET TO BE DISCOVERED. SOME MAY DIE, VANISH FROM THE WORLD WITHOUT OUR EVER KNOWING THEY HAD EXISTED.

One place where we are losing species at an enormous rate is in the oceans. Throughout the world, coral reefs, complex ecosystems that house a wide variety of plants and animals, are losing species that haven't even been discovered or identified. Coral reefs are made up of coral polyps, tiny, soft-bodied translucent animals related to sea anemones and jellyfish. Their hard skeletons are made of limestone, which attract certain other aquatic species that give the coral polyps their wide variety of rich colors. When the polyps attach themselves to rocks on the seafloor, they reproduce by dividing and growing, connecting to one another to create a colony that acts as a single organism. As colonies grow over hundreds and thousands of years, they join with other colonies and become reefs. Some of today's reefs started fifty million years ago.

AND THESE REEFS ARE DYING DUE TO THE THREE MAIN CULPRITS IN THE DEVASTATION OF THE WORLD'S OCEANS: OVERFISHING, POLLUTION, AND CLIMATE CHANGE.

THERE ARE ABOUT 20,000 KNOWN species of fish, though there may be many more we don't know about. Occasionally, a new fish is discovered. There may also be fish that are disappearing without our ever knowing that they existed.

Nothing is certain in the ocean. Fish that were said to be plentiful have suddenly disappeared. Fish that were said to be extinct have been discovered alive, most dramatically in 1938 when a coelacanth, a fish thought to have died out with the dinosaurs, turned up on the deck of a South African trawler. The list of 20,000 fish species that came out of the 1988 conference of biologists in which the term "biodiversity" was first coined is constantly being revised. Fish disappear and new ones are discovered.

COELACANTH
(*Latimeria chalumnae*)
Humorist Ogden Nash called the coelacanth "our only living fossil." Although it may seem like 20,000 known species of fish is a lot, it's actually not that big a number when considering that there are 550,000 known mollusk species and 751,000 known species of insects.

But there is one certainty. Something huge, a massive shifting in the natural order of the planet, is occurring in the oceans—and it will come with tremendous biological and social changes. This shift, the disappearance of species, is also happening on land. We are losing large numbers of species that inhabit tropical rain forests, for instance, because these are being cleared for people to live in or chopped down for lumber at un-precedented rates.

Mammals and reptiles all over the world seem to be vanishing. Some scientists have predicted that by the year 2100 up to 14 percent of all bird species may be extinct. And other scientists have concluded that one-fourth of all mammals, a third of amphibians, and 42 percent of all turtles and tortoise species also face extinction.

MEGAMOUTH
(*Megachasma pelagios*)

In 1976, the megamouth, a hitherto unknown species of shark, was discovered when the fourteen-foot-long 1,600-pound giant tried to eat the stabilizing anchor on a United States navy vessel near Hawaii.

A RECENT REPORT BY SCIENTISTS SAID THAT IF COMMERCIAL FISH SPECIES—THE FISH CAUGHT FOR FOOD—CONTINUE TO DECLINE AT THE CURRENT RATE, BY THE YEAR 2048 MOST COMMERCIAL FISH SPECIES WILL BE IN DANGER OF NEVER RECOVERING BECAUSE OF A LACK OF DIVERSITY IN THE OCEAN.

The United States government said in a 2002 study that one-third of the 274 most eaten types of fish are threatened by too much fishing. The United Nations Food and Agriculture Organization says this is true of almost two out of every three types of fish they have studied in the world. The oceans are in serious trouble.

THE STORY OF KRAM AND AILAT : PART 1

FOR HER 6TH BIRTHDAY, KRAM TOOK HIS DAUGHTER AILAT OCEAN FISHING FOR THE FIRST TIME. IT TURNED OUT TO BE QUITE AN ADVENTURE ...

BE CAREFUL, AILAT.

RRRRR

THEY CAME TO REST IN A CALM SPOT.

SHHH -- DO YOU HEAR THAT NOISE? IT'S A WHALE SINGING!

SUDDENLY, A LOUD SPLASH BROKE THE WATER'S SURFACE.

WOW!

THAT'S A HUMPBACK WHALE, AILAT! HE'S COMING UP TO PLAY!

THEY PATIENTLY WAITED FOR THE LARGE FISH TO CHASE THE SMALL ONES TO THE SURFACE.

NOW, DADDY?

WAIT FOR THE BIRDS TO SHOW US THAT THE FISH HAVE ARRIVED.

AND ...

NOW!

YOU CAUGHT A BIG ONE!

I WANT TO SHOW MOMMY!

SORRY, MY LITTLE SARDINE, THERE AREN'T ENOUGH OF THEM LEFT! WE'LL LET THIS ONE GO BACK TO HIS FAMILY.

AND SO KRAM & AILAT LET THEIR NEW FISH GO BACK INTO THE OCEAN.

TIME TO GO HOME, AILAT. DID YOU HAVE FUN?

I CAN'T WAIT TO GO FISHING AGAIN!

CHAPTER ONE

BEING A SHORT EXPOSITION ABOUT WHAT COULD HAPPEN AND HOW IT WOULD HAPPEN

And if these enemies or competitors be in the least degree favoured by any slight change of climate, they will increase in numbers, and, as each area is already fully stocked with inhabitants, the other species will decrease.

—Charles Darwin, On the Origin of Species

IT IS NOT LIKELY THAT HUMAN BEINGS COULD CATCH AND DESTROY ALL SEA LIFE EVEN IF THEY TRIED TO—AND, OF COURSE, WE ARE TRYING NOT TO. NEVERTHELESS, CONSIDERING OVERFISHING, POLLUTION, AND GLOBAL WARMING, THE ENTIRE SYSTEM OF OCEAN LIFE COULD COMPLETELY UNRAVEL WITHIN A RELATIVELY SHORT TIME—AND THEN WE WOULD BE HELPLESS SPECTATORS TO A CATACLYSM.

THE KEY TO SUCCESS FOR ALL LIFE ON EARTH is biodiversity, the presence of a wide variety of species. The more advanced species, the relatively recent arrivals, are the most complex. They are also the neediest species, more fragile than the less evolved species that have managed to survive for millions of years with few, if any, genetic changes.

The most highly evolved animals in the sea are mammals: whales, porpoises, and seals. Then come the fish that have backbones and fins. A fish with several fins is more evolved than a fish with one long fin. So a cod, for instance, which has three fins on top and three on the bottom, is more advanced than a flounder, which has only one long fin across the top and another across the bottom.

ATLANTIC COD
(*Gadus morhua*)

EUROPEAN FLOUNDER
(*Platichthys flesus*)

More advanced fish tend to feed on less advanced fish. Sometimes they help each other. Dolphins need the help of less advanced tuna to find the even less advanced smaller fish they both eat. Large fish often drive the small fish they eat to the surface, which makes it possible for seabirds that eat fish to feed. Those seabirds then deposit food on land that feeds crabs, beetles, and lizards, which in turn become food for land animals. So if the great variety of different species, the diversity, is reduced, it will become more difficult for the remaining animals to survive.

IF THE TOP FORTY SPECIES OF COMMERCIAL FISH WERE TO DISAPPEAR, OR EVEN HAVE THEIR POPULATIONS DECLINE TO VERY SMALL NUMBERS, THIS WOULD BE A GRAVE THREAT TO ALL OF BIODIVERSITY.

Other species would begin disappearing, too, either because their lives depended on cooperation with these species or because they used to eat those fish—or even because those vanished species used to hunt predators that were now free to roam and prosper. In time, all fin fish would disappear. In fact, most sea animals with backbones—vertebrates—would completely vanish. Their disappearance would mark the beginning of a process in which evolution goes in reverse. In the ocean, that would mean sea life returning to conditions 550 million years ago in a time known as the early Cambrian period—long before dinosaurs. At that time, there were no fish. Even today's small fish species, such as sardines and anchovies, are only 100 million years old.

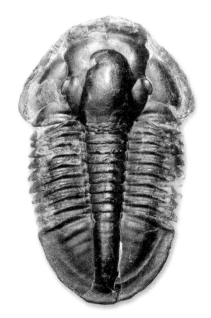

TRILOBITE
(*Elrathii kingii*)
Virtually all of the modern invertebrate groups appeared in the early Cambrian age, including worms, clams, snails, cephalopods, starfish, urchins, crabs, lobsters, insects, and trilobites.

ONCE THE LARGER, MORE-EVOLVED FISH WERE GONE, SOME MAMMALS WOULD DIE OFF VERY QUICKLY. THE DOLPHIN, FOR INSTANCE, WOULD NOT FIND ITS FOOD BECAUSE THE BLUEFIN TUNA IT USED TO DEPEND ON WOULD BE GONE.

ATLANTIC BLUEFIN TUNA
(*Thunnus thynnus*)
Schools of tuna are known to swim near or alongside dolphins for protection against predators, such as sharks.

The seal would simply starve. (Elephant seals might last longer, however, because they feed on squid, a primitive invertebrate that would survive the rapid extinction of marine life.) Humpback whales and other large mammals that feed on the tiny shrimp called krill would also survive for a while, because they can travel thousands of miles looking for food; but since they need older whales to tell them the location of the feeding grounds, and they would likely end up competing with humans for krill to eat, eventually they would die, too.

WITHOUT LARGE BOTTOM FISH TO DRIVE THE SMALL FISH TO THE SURFACE, SEABIRDS WOULD DIE OUT.

This has already started to happen in some places. Gulls and terns have been vanishing from the Atlantic at an alarming rate because of a loss of fish from the upper level of the water.

Seabirds would actually be an exception to the pattern of the most evolved dying off first. Some of the most highly evolved tropical seabirds seem peculiarly built for a world with a scarcity of prey. The newest models—new in terms of millions of years— have very small, underdeveloped feet (because they don't land very much), but they have

ATLANTIC PUFFIN
(*Fratercula arctica*)
Puffins eat sand eels, two-inch-thin silvery fish. Recently, sand eels have been used to feed farmed fish (see Chapter Seven), so they've been taken by the hundreds of thousands from the ocean. A huge sand eel fishery in the North Sea near Scotland that supplies fish farms has been blamed for a decline in seabirds, such as puffins and kittiwakes.

very well designed, long wings that effortlessly sustain flight for long periods of time. Tropical seabirds fly great distances in search of prey. Frigate birds can stay in flight for months. They're graceful fliers—but very awkward on land—that would probably survive for a while because, though much of their food consists of fish (they harass gulls and other birds to disgorge their meals), they also eat jellyfish. Sooty terns, also with long, thin wings, can stay in flight up to six years, traveling long distances and scooping fish driven to the surface. Sooty terns like to feed on flying fish. The problem with these flying feeders is that once they locate prey, they dive into a school and the fish swim deeper—so a sooty tern's only chance to feed is if the fish are driven to the surface by predator fish below. If those are gone, so are the sooty terns' chances of survival.

JUAN FERNÁNDEZ PETREL
(*Pteroderma externa*)
This species of petrel, endemic to Chile, is now on several endangered watch lists.

Birds also look for tuna, dolphin, whales, and other large fish to help them find their food. The classic example is the petrel from the Juan Fernández Islands off of Chile, which are famous as the site of the Robinson Crusoe story. These birds rely on the spinner dolphin and eastern yellowtail tuna to lead them to baitfish. The petrel is entirely dependent on subsurface predators—the larger fish from below—and so despite its great capacity to search for food because of its strong, long wings, it would also be doomed by the destruction of the more evolved fish.

IN THE END, THERE WOULD BE FEW SURVIVORS IN THE OCEAN.

One survivor would probably be plankton, the tiny creatures that so many animals feed on. The total population of plankton and krill is already the largest mass of protein in the world today. Without these other ocean creatures around to eat them and keep their numbers in check, the sea would become clogged with plankton, which would probably turn the ocean either pink or orange. Overpopulated, large numbers of plankton would die, leaving poisonous areas the size of small islands where they are rotting. The poison would kill off shellfish and animals, including mammals that eat the shellfish. This has already begun to happen, and more and more shellfish beds have been closed periodically because of these harmful algal blooms, which are sometimes referred to as "red tides." But the sea could become one enormous red tide.

HARMFUL ALGAL BLOOM
Harmful algal blooms, which are also known as red tides, like this one off the coast of Alaska, appear to be increasing worldwide, according to the National Oceanic and Atmospheric Administration (NOAA).

ANOTHER SURVIVOR WOULD BE THE JELLYFISH. THIS ANCIENT SPECIES DATES BACK MORE THAN 500 MILLION YEARS TO THE CAMBRIAN PERIOD. THE JELLYFISH IS ACTUALLY A VERY HIGHLY EVOLVED TYPE OF PLANKTON. IT IS THE COCKROACH OF THE SEA, AN ANIMAL LITTLE LOVED BY HUMAN BEINGS BUT PARTICULARLY WELL DESIGNED FOR SURVIVAL.

We don't think much of jellyfish because, like insects, they are not even in our phylum. But whether we love them or not, jellyfish are an evolutionary success, likely to survive when more evolved animals fail. They can eat an unusually broad range of foods, and if they can't find enough to eat, they can make themselves smaller so that they will need less food. They are also resistant to poisoning, and have the ability to grow new animals from parts of their body.

NOMURA JELLYFISH
(*Nemopilema nomurai*)
In recent years, more and more outbreaks of overwhelming quantities of jellyfish have been reported around the world. The most striking incident was the recent invasion of the Sea of Japan by large numbers of Nomura jellyfish, which are six feet wide and weigh more than one hundred pounds.

Jellyfish populations are kept under control by the 124 species of fish and thirty-four other animals that eat jellyfish. But if their enemies were to disappear, the jellyfish population would greatly expand. Its zooplankton food supply would be made almost limitless by the lack of other animals to eat them.

And because warmth also stimulates jellyfish growth, global warming would help the jellyfish reproduce. And in this scenario, not only would evolution start going in reverse, but parts of the food chain could start reversing, too. Animals that were hunted could turn around and start eating their hunters. If the jellyfish population expanded while the fish populations were declining, jellyfish might start eating some of the fish that once ate them. A jellyfish eats by stinging its prey with its tentacles and then feeding it into its floating belly, which acts as a kind of pump that gives it the ability to travel through water.

THE TAKEOVER OF THE WORLD BY JELLYFISH HAS GOOD POTENTIAL FOR A SCI-FI THRILLER, BUT IT IS NOT THAT FAR-FETCHED AND VERY LIKELY TO HAPPEN IN A WORLD WITHOUT FISH.

A jellyfish snack? In about sixty years, jellyfish might be your only choice if you're in the mood for seafood. Though not a popular food for Westerners, the Chinese have eaten jellyfish since ancient times. In Asia, about 425 thousand tons of jellyfish are caught every year. This is an example of a light jellyfish salad.

JELLYFISH SALAD

- ½ pound shredded prepared jellyfish
- 2 teaspoons light soy sauce
- 3 tablespoons sesame oil
- 2 teaspoons white rice vinegar
- 2 teaspoons sugar
- 3 tablespoons toasted white sesame seeds

Bring a pot of water to a boil. Rinse the jellyfish well in cold running water and let it drain. Place the jellyfish into the boiling water, but turn off the heat and allow it to stand for about 15 minutes, until tender. Drain and soak for 5 minutes in fresh cold water, and repeat this five more times. Drain thoroughly. Blot dry with paper towels. Then set aside.

Blend soy sauce, sesame oil, rice vinegar, and sugar. Dress the jellyfish with this sauce and toss thoroughly 30 minutes before serving. Immediately before serving, add the sesame seeds.

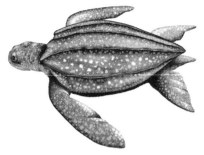

LEATHERBACK TURTLE
(*Dermochelys coriacea*)

Leatherback turtles are the largest of living sea turtles. Although an adult can weigh up to 2 tons and measure 8 feet long, hatchlings are only 2½ inches long, leaving them vulnerable to predators. The United States has listed leatherbacks as an endangered species and conservation organizations around the world are trying to protect them.

A few other animals might also profit from this turn of events. Leatherback turtles would do well. Like the jellyfish, which is their primary food, they are an ancient species—older than most fish. Their diet is almost exclusively jellyfish. They have nearly disappeared because people like to eat them, but in a sea full of jellyfish, they would do quite well. But with no fish left to eat, humans might start going after leatherbacks—and even jellyfish—for food, so their chances of survival might not be great in the long haul.

As evolution reversed itself, worse things than jellyfish would flourish, including prehistoric bacteria. Already, little-known prehistoric organisms have emerged in nearly a dozen places around the globe—bacteria that prospered 2.7 billion years ago have been plaguing fishermen in recent years in the form of hairy-looking growths that constrict the throat, making breathing difficult and causing severe welts on the skin. Who knows what other bacteria would flourish in a warm, swampy, orange ocean full of jellyfish and plankton?

THE TRAGEDY OF THE SEAS, MUCH OF WHICH HAS ITS ROOTS ON LAND, WOULD SOON SPREAD TO LAND. WITH SEABIRDS GONE, THE REPTILES, LIZARDS, INSECTS, AND CRABS THAT ATE THE FOOD DISCARDED BY SEABIRDS WOULD DIE OUT, TOO.

A decline in seabirds would therefore lead to a decline in lizards, crabs, and beetles. The absence of those creatures would lead to the decline of some freshwater fish. And this would eventually impact land-based mammals, including us.

There are many things that are scary about the idea of evolution reversing itself, but the scariest is that we, the *Homo sapiens*, are latecomers to the evolution game. In the 500 million years of life on Earth, we only arrived about ten million years ago. So if the chain of life unraveled and evolution went backward, we would not be among the survivors.

THIS, OF COURSE, IS A WORST-CASE SCENARIO— WHAT COULD HAPPEN IF WE DID ABSOLUTELY NOTHING. THE GOOD PART ABOUT IMAGINING WHAT COULD HAPPEN IS THAT WE CAN MOVE TO TRY TO PREVENT IT FROM HAPPENING. HOW? BY CHANGING THE WAY WE DO THINGS NOW.

AND WE HAVE THE POWER TO DO THAT—NOW. BUT BEFORE WE KNOW WHAT TO CHANGE AND HOW TO CHANGE IT, WE NEED TO UNDERSTAND HOW WE GOT INTO THIS PREDICAMENT IN THE FIRST PLACE.

KRAM

AILAT

ONE DAY, KRAM WENT OUT ON HIS FRIEND SERAFINO'S FISHING BOAT. SERAFINO AND HIS SONS, FRANK AND SALVY, WERE COMMERCIAL FISHERMEN.

YOU SHOULD BE FISHING WITH A ROD INSTEAD OF NETS, SERAFINO!

KRAM, I HAVE TO MAKE A LIVING!

YOU WON'T BE ABLE TO, WHEN ALL THE FISH ARE GONE!

SERAFINO ORDERED FRANK & SALVY TO BRING UP THE NETS. BIRDS CIRCLED AND DOVE AT THE BOAT, TRYING TO TAKE THE FISH.

MOST BIRDS I'VE EVER SEEN!

THAT'S BECAUSE YOU'RE TAKING TOO MANY FISH!

FRANK & SALVY BEGAN TO THROW BACK THE DEAD FLOUNDER THAT THEY CAUGHT, BECAUSE THEY HAD REACHED THE LEGAL LIMIT OF WHAT THEY COULD TAKE. KRAM AND SERAFINO CONTINUED TO ARGUE ...

WHAT DOES IT ACCOMPLISH TO THROW BACK DEAD FISH, ANYWAY?

THE WHOLE SYSTEM IS OUT OF BALANCE, SERAFINO. IT'S A DISASTER!

IT'S TRUE THAT THERE ARE FEWER SEAGULLS AND COD, BUT THERE ARE MORE HERRING AND HADDOCK THAN EVER!

IF WE RE-ORDER THE FOOD CHAIN, THE WHOLE THING COULD COLLAPSE!

WHY ARE YOU ALWAYS THIS WAY, KRAM?

SOON, THE SUN BEGAN TO SET. SERAFINO HAD THE NETS BROUGHT UP ONE LAST TIME, AS THEY HEADED BACK TO THE DOCKS

KRAM, YOU'LL FORGET ALL OF THIS TONIGHT WHEN WE'RE FEASTING ON HALIBUT!

WHEN THEY ARRIVED ON SHORE, KRAM CALLED AILAT IN FROM THE BEACH, WHERE SHE WAS CHASING CRABS.

AILAT, DINNER TIME!

THAT EVENING, OVER DINNER ...

DON'T WORRY, KRAM. FISHERMEN ARE CAREFUL NOT TO TAKE TOO MANY FISH.

I'M NOT SURE, SERAFINO. I FEEL LIKE I NEED TO WARN EVERYONE.

I UNDERSTAND, MY FRIEND. LET'S EAT!

CAPTAIN LEO'S

WILL YOU CUT THIS HALIBUT STEAK FOR ME, DADDY?

OF COURSE I WILL, MY LITTLE SARDINE!

TO BE CONTINUED ...

CHAPTER TWO

BEING THE TRUE STORY OF HOW HUMANS FIRST BEGAN TO FISH AND HOW FISHING BECAME AN INDUSTRY

Nor ought we to think that the occasional destruction of an animal of any particular color would produce little effect.
—Charles Darwin, On the Origin of Species

ONCE THE ORDER OF NATURE IS UNDERSTOOD, THAT ALL LIFE STRUGGLES FOR SURVIVAL AND IS INTERCONNECTED WITH THE REST OF LIFE, IT BECOMES CLEAR THAT FISHERMEN TAKING FISH FROM THE SEA ALWAYS HAD AN IMPACT ON MARINE LIFE.

WHEN THE DESTRUCTION OF FISH WAS moderate, the impact was moderate, and the small adjustments made by nature usually were not even noticed. It is only when the destruction of fish takes place on a large scale that we start to see enormous changes in the order of sea life.

Before human beings could write down their history, they recorded their lives by drawing pictures, often on the walls of caves. Most of these drawings illustrate the hunting of land animals. Only very rarely are fish depicted. But the fossilized remains of fish bones and fishhooks show that fishing, though not one of the first activities, began quite early. Fish lines and nets were made from vegetable fibers. Hooks were made from bones. Fish were also sometimes speared, and if you ever try this you will see that it takes tremendous skill to get only one fish.

Fishing was a game of fishermen tricking fish, finding new and better ways to catch fish. The fisherman who caught the most fish was the best fisherman—and the richest one. Throughout history—until fifteen to twenty years ago—fishermen saw their job as doing whatever they could to catch as many fish as possible. But they understood that the secret of their game was to catch as many fish as they could while still maintaining a prosperous fish population in their fishing

"Fishing grounds" refers to an area of water that is good for fishing.

grounds. They knew that if they fished too much, the fish would all swim away. They worried that putting out too many nets would keep the fish from coming in, and they also understood that taking too many small, young fish would destroy the population.

UNLIKE HUMANS AND OTHER MAMMALS, FISH CONTINUE TO GROW BIGGER THROUGHOUT THEIR LIVES. THE BIGGER THE FISH, THE MORE EGGS IT CAN LAY, AND THE MORE YOUNG FISH IT WILL PRODUCE. SO IT IS IMPORTANT TO ALLOW SMALL FISH TO GROW LARGE. EVEN A THOUSAND YEARS AGO, FISHERMEN UNDERSTOOD THIS.

Until modern times, fishermen and fishing communities worried most about migratory fish. These fish usually live in the middle level of the ocean as opposed to "ground fish" that live on or near the ocean floor. Herring is an example of a migratory fish. It was an extremely important fish to northern Europe in the Middle Ages because back then, before refrigeration, fish that were most valuable were those that could be preserved well in salt. Herring was such a fish. It could be pickled in salted water, put in barrels, and, if packed well, these barrels could be shipped to faraway places.

. A woodcut from the *Ortus Sanitatis* published in 1491 depicts a fishmonger gutting herring and the kind of barrels into which herring were packed and shipped.

A village might fish for herring in a nearby area for twenty years, always bringing in huge numbers of fish. And then suddenly the fish would be gone, plunging the once-prosperous village into poverty. What happened to the herring? In the Middle Ages, it was often believed that God had sent the herring away as punishment for people living immoral lives. When a village lost their school of herring, it was disgraced. Some took a more "scientific" view—at least for those times. They feared that fishermen farther out in the ocean were using too many nets and the herring were not able to swim into their fishing grounds. Netting was always seen as dangerous.

ATLANTIC HERRING
(*Clupea harengus*)
One of the most populous fish on Earth, herring are known for having enormous schools of fish—sometimes numbering in the hundreds of thousands.

But in reality what probably had happened was that subtle shifts in the order of nature had taken place. As Darwin noted, migration is an important factor. The herring that lived in the middle level of the ocean might have abandoned their fishing grounds because too many of the fish at the bottom of the ocean, which ate herring, had moved into the area. Or the herring might have gone because the smaller fish that they ate were leaving, and they followed them in search of food. Or maybe too many birds had driven the herring away, or had driven some other types of fish that ate the same things as herring into the herring fishing grounds, which in turn had driven the herring away. Or it just might have been a combination of all these factors put together over time.

IT WAS IN THE NINETEENTH CENTURY that fishermen first started to play a major role in the shifts in the natural order of the sea. Not until then did the changes fishermen were making in the sea become threatening to the entire order of life. The real trouble began when the invention of engine power was applied to commercial fishing.

Thomas Savery, an English military engineer and inventor, patented the first steam engine in 1698. Savery was trying to pump water out of coal mines. His machine consisted of a closed vessel filled with water, into which steam was injected under pressure. It seems a simple device, but it employed a world-changing idea: heat applied to water creates steam that pushes outward, creating the energy to move objects. Steam engines were not used on ships until a century later, though— and even then, this technology was not applied to fishing.

FISHERMEN TEND TO BE PROBLEM SOLVERS BY NATURE, AND UNTIL THERE IS A PROBLEM TO SOLVE, THEY ARE NOT PARTICULARLY INTERESTED IN NEW TECHNOLOGY (ALTHOUGH ONCE THERE IS A PROBLEM TO SOLVE, THEY CAN BE EXTREMELY INNOVATIVE).

Because the most productive fishing grounds in the world at the time, those of the North Atlantic, yielded so many fish for the fishermen—even though they were on sailing ships that were wind powered, there was no reason for them to switch to engine-powered ships. In fact, sail power worked so well for fishing, that in New England it was used until the 1950s! Even today, sail power is still used by fishermen in poorer countries.

It was in the North Sea in the late nineteenth century that innovations in fishing began to take place. The North Sea is a body of water rich in fish, which is surrounded by the great European fishing nations, such as Scotland, England, France, Belgium, The Netherlands, Denmark, Germany, Sweden, and Norway. Throughout history, these nations competed with one another for fish and fishing territories. Some of these countries had even gone to war over it: Holland and England battled over North Sea herring during the Anglo-Dutch wars of the seventeenth century; France and England fought over North American cod in the early eighteenth century during the Queen Anne's War.

For centuries, North Sea nations kept bringing in larger and larger catches, with little sign of any decline in the supply of fish. In the early seventeenth century, the Dutch had two thousand ships in the North Sea fishing for herring. The British responded by banning foreign fishing vessels within fourteen miles of the British coastline (this was the distance visible from the top of a mast).

IT WAS THE BRITISH THAT FIRST started using a beam trawler in the fourteenth century. Also called a "wondrychoum," this was a net suspended from a beam and dragged through the sea.

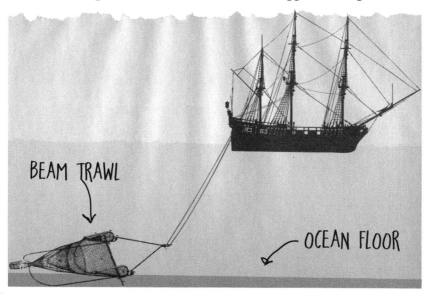

BEAM TRAWL

OCEAN FLOOR

DIAGRAM OF A SAIL-POWERED VESSEL
DRAGGING A BEAM TRAWL

It was fishermen themselves who first spoke out about the dangers of using beam trawlers to catch fish. In 1376, they petitioned the British Parliament to pass a law banning their use because the nets swept up fish indiscriminately, taking many immature young fish. Parliament did not institute a ban. Then, in the seventeenth century, Scottish fishermen petitioned Charles I to protect fishing from "the great destruction made of fish by a net or engine now called the Trawle."

In 1874, the "otter trawl" was invented. First used by the British, this net had no beam hanging off the ship but instead had "doors," flat slabs of wood or iron on either side of the net, that caused the sides to stay open. But the otter trawl only worked at a constant speed, requiring a more reliable and more powerful source of energy than wind and sails. Steam power was needed for an efficient otter trawl. In 1876, a fishing vessel was launched with a steam-powered capstan, a rotary device for hauling the nets in and out, and, in 1881, a vessel was launched that used steam power as an auxiliary to sails. The ship could sail to the fishing grounds but then use engine power when dragging the nets. But even with the dual energy, it did not have enough power to drag nets efficiently in open seas or deep water.

The problem with beam trawlers was that sailing ships didn't have the power to haul huge nets—if the nets were too large and caught too many fish, they would be too heavy to pull so they had to use small ones.

On the other hand, beam trawlers were quite efficient in other ways. The potential of dragging a net through the water and hauling up everything in its path had obvious advantages over setting lines with baited hooks. In addition to requiring no bait, a beam trawler seemed certain to haul in a much higher percentage of the fish it passed. By 1774, beam trawling had become one of the principal fishing techniques in the North Sea.

IN THE MID-NINETEENTH CENTURY, new ideas were aimed at improving the quality of fish, and of getting the fish to market fresher. Well boats came into use. These were ships that contained a tank of seawater into which the caught fish would be dumped, enabling fish to stay fresh longer than previously. This meant that fishermen could remain at sea, fishing for a longer period of time. Once the quality of fish improved in

England, and most notably in London, the demand for fish rapidly increased.

Then in 1848, a new dramatic technological advance was created in the port of Grimsby on the North Sea at the mouth of the Humber River: a rail connection straight to London. Because it was a large port, capable of storing ice from not-too-distant Norway (ice was essential for keeping fish fresh on its way to market), the port of Grimsby became a premier port for quality fish in London. In 1881, the *Zodiac*, the first vessel built for dragging fishing nets under steam power, was launched from Grimsby.

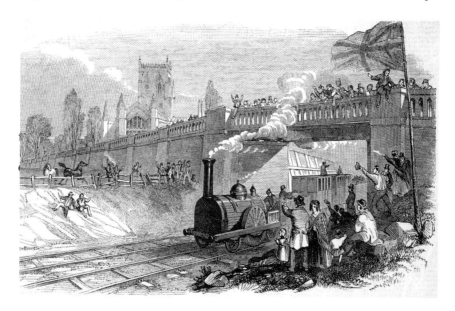

THE FIRST LOCOMOTIVE PASSES THROUGH THE PORT OF GRIMSBY
(ILLUSTRATED LONDON NEWS PRINT LIBRARY COLLECTION, 1848)

Dragging nets from engine-powered (as opposed to wind-powered) ships was a huge technological boon for the fishermen, especially because they could then use the rail line at Grimsby to get the fish to London rapidly. Soon, a rail line and port system were organized: The boats would stay fishing in the North Sea for as long as ten weeks at a time, all the while off-loading their catch to the fleet's carriers, which sped the fish to Grimsby. This system was used until 1901, just a little over a century ago. The southern part of the North Sea is an extremely shallow body of water, which is why it was once so rich in fish, and the boats worked primarily on the even more shallow Dogger Bank, which was teeming with fish.

Even though steam-powered vessels had been around for almost eighty years, and were proving to be lucrative for the fishermen that used them, by the 1870s most fishermen were still using sail power. Over the next ten years, however, four things happened:

1. STEAM ENGINES GOT MORE POWERFUL AND BECAME CAPABLE OF DRAGGING FOUR TIMES AS DEEP AS THE SAIL-POWERED DRAGGERS.

2. MORE POWERFUL STEAM ENGINES OPENED UP NEW GROUNDS TO DRAGGING, INCLUDING THE DEEPER, NORTHERN PART OF THE NORTH SEA AS WELL AS THE WATERS AROUND ICELAND.

3. BRITAIN BECAME THE GREATEST FISHING NATION IN THE WORLD IN TERMS OF TONS OF FISH LANDED.

4. THE FISH STOCK OF THE NORTH SEA STARTED SHOWING SIGNS OF A VANISHING FISH POPULATION.

THE FISHING WAS SO GOOD THAT FISHERMEN DIDN'T WORRY TOO MUCH ABOUT THE DECLINE IN THE OLD FISHING GROUNDS: THEY SIMPLY MOVED ON TO NEW ONES.

Their new boats could fish in places sailing vessels couldn't before, so they were less dependent on the rapidly thinning traditional fishing grounds. The whole world was opening to them.

That resulted in a very significant change: In the North Sea, the drop-off in catches after ten years of dragging was dramatic. Scientists began to grow concerned. From the late 1870s on, the English regularly convened commissions aimed at curbing the destruction caused by trawlers. In the meanwhile, though, the size, capacity, and numbers of such vessels were increasing at a steady pace.

Even Gloucester, Massachusetts, which was not only the oldest fishing port in the United States but was famous for having invented its own kind of sail-powered fishing boat, the schooner, got its first beam trawler in the 1890s.

Fishermen feared the devastating consequences the continued use of net trawlers would bring. By 1911, New England fishermen were uniting with those of other regions to demand that congress ban the new practices.

The government, unfortunately, never acted, but it is clear that the ensuing tragedy of the next hundred years was plainly predicted back in 1911. A *Gloucester Daily Times* article at the time stated that there was a feeling, not only in Gloucester but in other New England ports, that "something should and must be done," and that "the continued operation of these trawlers scraping over the fishing grounds and destroying countless numbers of young and immature fish, is the greatest menace to the future of the fisheries, the greatest danger the fisheries have ever faced along this coast."

"THE GREATEST DANGER." IT WAS ALL UNDERSTOOD A CENTURY AGO. GLOUCESTER FISHERMEN SIMPLY HAD TO LOOK AT EUROPE — AND ESPECIALLY GREAT BRITAIN — TO SEE THE FUTURE.

According to this article, beam trawling had increased the fishing capacity in the North Sea to 14 thousand times the capacity of the former sailing fleet. The article claimed the "wasteful destruction of immature fish," was one of the primary problems and that this destruction "cannot be obviated by regulating the size of the mesh nor by returning the undersized fish caught to the sea." The article concluded—as American and European regulators have only recently come to understand—that "the only feasible method is to close off fishing grounds or prohibit the landing of fish."

The *Gloucester Daily Times* article further asserted that the history of the British fisheries showed that if New England did not ban trawling in its infancy, the trawler owners and the businessmen who made a living off the trawlers would later on become too powerful to stop.

In the twentieth century, steam power was abandoned for oil power, namely gasoline and diesel. The submarine technology used in World War II led to new ideas for fishing. Where naval ships had been chasing submarines underwater, now fishermen could chase fish underwater using similar methods: small airplanes could be sent out to find the schools of fish, and sonar—sound that radiated and bounced off of objects, which it then identified—could also be used to find fish.

Nets were also made more effective. Originally, a net could not drag off the bottom of the ocean because it would tear on the rocky subterrain, which would cause fishermen to lose their costly net. But the invention of plastic during World War II changed that: now a strong, inexpensive plastic cord, called a monofilament, made netting much cheaper, so fishermen could risk dragging right on the seafloor.

There were other inventions, such as "ticklers," chains on the bottom of the net, that had a lot of movement and drove fish into the net. "Rock hoppers," bouncy rubber rollers that could hop over and between rocks were developed to scrape the bottom more closely. Bottom draggers could now go anywhere because rock hoppers and monofilament nets made it unnecessary to avoid rough, jagged bottoms. FISHERMEN COULD HUNT DOWN FISH AS THEY HID BETWEEN ROCKS BECAUSE THERE WAS LITERALLY NOWHERE LEFT FOR FISH TO HIDE, AND FISHERMEN COULD DO IT FASTER THAN EVER WITH THE GAS-POWERED TRAWLERS, TEARING UP THE BOTTOM AS THEY WENT, COMPLETELY CHANGING THE OCEAN HABITAT FOREVER.

WHEN AILAT TURNED 8 YEARS OLD, KRAM TOOK HER TO THE CARIBBEAN TO LEARN TO SNORKEL.

WAIT UNTIL YOU SEE ALL THE COLORFUL FISH THAT LIVE IN THE CORAL REEF, AILAT!

KRAM TAUGHT AILAT ABOUT ALL THE DIFFERENT FISH THEY SAW.

DADDY, I SAW A QUEEN ANGELFISH!

ARE YOU SURE, AILAT? I ONLY SAW GRAY ANGELFISH.

YES, IT WAS BRIGHT BLUE AND HAD A YELLOW TAIL!

WHEN THEY FINISHED SNORKELING, KRAM SPOTTED A FISHERMAN ON THE BEACH, SELLING THE DAY'S CATCH.

LOOK, AILAT. A CARIBBEAN FISHERMAN! LET'S SEE WHAT HE'S CAUGHT TODAY.

FRESH FISH

AS THEY GOT CLOSER, KRAM NOTICED SOMETHING ODD...

WHY ARE YOU SELLING PARROT FISH? NO ONE EATS THOSE.

THEY DO NOW, MAN.

TODAY: PARROT FISH

THE FISHERMAN EXPLAINED.

ALL THE OTHER FISH HAVE GONE AWAY -- THIS IS WHAT WE HAVE.

THE PARROT FISH EAT ALGAE, THOUGH... WITHOUT THEM, THE BEACH WOULD BE COVERED IN IT.

RELAX, MAN. A LITTLE SEAWEED WON'T HURT YOU.

KRAM TRIED TO WARN HIM, BUT IT WAS NO USE.

YOU DON'T UNDERSTAND, THE ALGAE WILL CHOKE THE REEF!

YOU THINK LIKE A RICH MAN. HOW AM I SUPPOSED TO MAKE A LIVING?

TO BE CONTINUED...

CHAPTER THREE

BEING THE SAD, CAUTIONARY TALE OF THE ORANGE ROUGHY

The amount of food for each species, of course,

gives the extreme limit to which each can increase.

—Charles Darwin, ON THE ORIGIN OF SPECIES

IF YOU LOOK AT A MAP OF THE WORLD OR A GLOBE AND SEE HOW TWO-THIRDS OF THE EARTH IS COVERED BY OCEAN, YOU MIGHT IMAGINE THAT THERE ARE A LOT MORE FISH IN THE WORLD THAN THERE REALLY ARE. THAT IS EXACTLY WHAT MOST PEOPLE DID THINK FOR MANY YEARS.

THE OCEAN THAT FISHERMEN KNEW was full of fish—but that was because they did not go very far. Sea life, as with land life, depends on sunlight. Wherever the sea is strongly penetrated by sunlight, vegetable nutrients grow. The area becomes rich in nitrates, which stimulates the growth of plankton. Plankton is really a grouping of many tiny plants and animals, some of them only one cell, that drift in the sea. Some, such as phytoplankton, are plants, others, such as zooplankton, are animals. Phytoplankton, floating plants, come in many types and shapes, but are so small that they can only be seen through a microscope. Like land-based plants, they are green because they are filled with a substance called chlorophyll, which uses energy from sunlight to create sugars for food, which, in turn, creates oxygen. This process, which sustains plant life on earth, is called photosynthesis. It is a very old system created some 3.5 billion years ago when the only living organisms were microscopic and the earth was full of gases. Phytoplankton are found where the sunlight penetrates the sea, and since this is the beginning of the sea's food chain, this is where the most life is found.

Because there are so many phytoplankton, there are huge numbers of a slightly larger creature called zooplankton, which eat phytoplankton. Zooplankton range in size

In addition to phytoplankton and zooplankton, there's another type of plankton called a mixotroph. Mixotrophs are zooplankton that are both plants, which feed by photosynthesis, and animals, which eat and swallow food.

from microscopic to almost eight inches. Some zooplankton are actually larvae that eventually change into worms, mollusks, crustaceans, coral, and even some types of fish. They also help to control one of the earliest forms of life: bacteria.

A sea with plentiful zooplankton provides plentiful food for tiny, shrimplike creatures called krill. Krill are one of the smallest forms of sea life that humans actually eat, though they're so small most people don't even bother with them. This is a good thing because much sea life depends on krill, and these creatures would not do well if they had to compete with humans for food. Herring eat krill, for instance, as do giant humpback whales.

SEVERAL TIMES THE SIZE OF AN ELEPHANT, THE HUMPBACK WHALE IS ONE OF THE LARGEST MAMMALS ON EARTH—AND YET IT FEEDS ON ONE OF THE TINIEST FORMS OF LIFE IN THE WORLD.

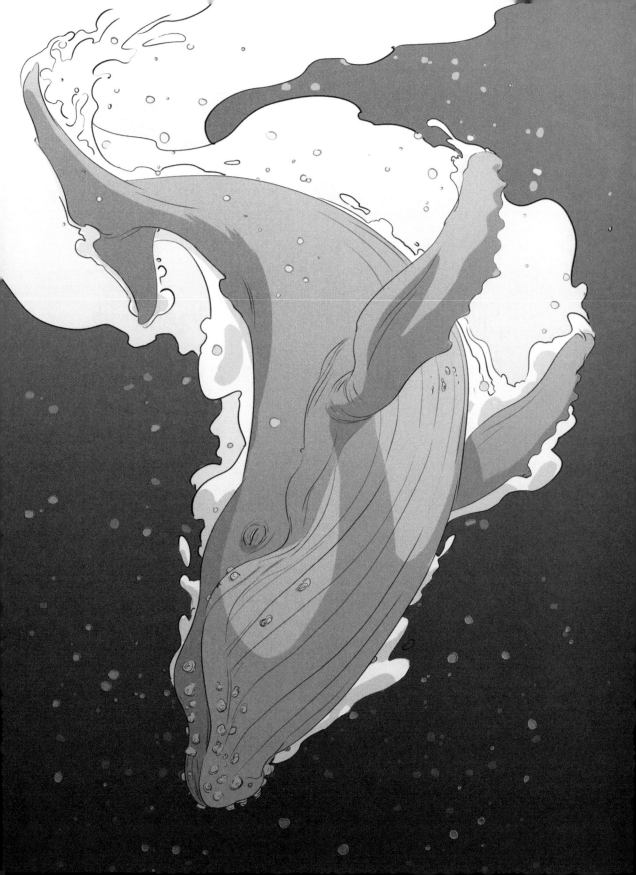

SOME FISH SWIM NEAR THE BOTTOM of the ocean and can swim up to eat smaller fish or down to eat the shellfish living at the seafloor. These are slow, steady hunters who stay close to home and whose muscles constitute the white meat that most people prefer to eat. Fish with white meat, such as

COD, HADDOCK, FLOUNDER, AND HALIBUT, ARE THE MOST APPRECIATED AND THE HIGHEST-PRICED FISH AVAILABLE.

But there are also fish that swim in the middle water just a little below the surface—fast, hard-swimming animals who sometimes travel long distances. These fish, such as sardines, anchovies, herring, mackerel, and even a few large fish such as tuna, have muscles that are darker and flesh that's a little oilier than the white-meat fish. By netting large quantities of these cheaper fish, a fisherman could still earn a good living. The smaller of these middle-water fish, which feed on krill that feed on zooplankton that feed on phytoplankton, are eaten by the larger white-meat fish on the bottom. Trying to escape hungry predators, such as cod, the smaller fish from the middle depths swim to the surface for safety—and that's just where seabirds swoop down and eat them.

Darwin was right. A healthy ecosystem is based on the destruction of life and the struggles for survival among species, and it is in such systems that men in the form of fishermen are drawn to take part in the killing. Ninety percent of the fishing they do is within 200 miles of land.

The base of the original North American fishing industry was established in the seventeenth century. For centuries, the Grand Banks, a series of wide shoals, shallow patches of ocean, running about one hundred miles offshore along the Atlantic coast, from Newfoundland to New England, were especially rich with bottom-dwelling fish, such as cod and halibut. The ports of St. John's in Newfoundland and Gloucester in Massachusetts were established because of their nearness to the Grand Banks, and Boston became an important port by trading the salted cod caught on the banks. The Flemish Cap, which is more than 350 miles from the nearest ports, is the farthest of the banks, while the Grand Bank, which is larger than Newfoundland, is the biggest. Georges Bank, the southernmost bank off of New England, is larger than Massachusetts.

FARTHER OUT TO SEA, THERE IS LIFE AND THERE ARE FISH. BUT MANY OF THEM LIVE AT GREAT DEPTHS THAT HAVE NOT BEEN EXPLORED BECAUSE UNTIL RECENTLY WE DIDN'T HAVE THE ABILITY TO REACH THAT FAR BELOW THE SURFACE.

Most attempts to commercialize fish hauled in from farther out at sea have proven disastrous in a very short time because of our lack of understanding of this deepwater life system.

THE ORANGE ROUGHY IS AN EXCELLENT EXAMPLE.

ORANGE ROUGHY
(*Hoplostethus atlanticus*)

The orange roughy gets its name from the orange color it turns after it dies. When it's alive, it's actually red. The fact that it is named after its appearance when dead shows that few have ever seen it alive. It is a large species in a family of deepwater fish known as Trachichthyidae, or slimeheads. It was first found in the western Pacific, where it lives in cold water at depths as great as 5,000 feet.

Fishermen were not capable of reaching the orange roughy until the 1970s, but once they did, eating orange roughy became fashionable in Australia, the United States, and many other places in the world well into the 1990s.

IT WAS NOT UNDERSTOOD THAT THIS SPECIES WAS NOT LIKE OTHER FISH WE HAD KNOWN.

For one thing, many scientists think that an orange roughy lives for 150 years, which is at least five times as long as most of the fish we know. The age is disputed, with some saying it lives even longer, but the problem with this long-lived species is that it grows very slowly. The fish doesn't even become capable of producing offspring until it is twenty years old, which would be an older fish in most of the species we know. This means that many orange roughy that appear to be mature are actually quite young and haven't yet reproduced.

THE LARGE-SCALE KILLING OF FISH THAT HAVEN'T YET REPRODUCED WILL IN TIME DESTROY THEM, AND THAT'S EXACTLY WHAT HAPPENED TO THE ORANGE ROUGHY POPULATIONS

off New Zealand and Australia, where the fish was first discovered. After little more than ten years, the Australian orange roughy population was only 10 percent of what it had been in the 1990s. So fishermen went looking somewhere else for this popular new species, and found it in the Atlantic Ocean off southern Africa, as well as farther north from Morocco to Iceland. Just as it happened with the Australian orange roughy, these populations very quickly showed signs of vanishing.

THE SAD STORY OF HOW THE ORANGE ROUGHY BECAME ONE OF THE WORLD'S MOST THREATENED FISH POPULATIONS WITHIN DECADES OF BEING DISCOVERED BY US

should serve as a caution to what could happen. Who knows what years of dragging nets through these deep unknown oceans is doing to deepwater ecosystems—we are probably damaging and destroying species we haven't even discovered yet and will never know about. It would follow the laws of Darwin if it turned out that rare fish in hard-to-reach places had fewer chances of survival than large populations of more familiar fish living in ideal environments closer to shore.

THE STORY OF KRAM AND AILAT : PART 4

Panel 1: ONE DAY, KRAM WAS INVITED ON TELEVISION TO TALK ABOUT THE FUTURE OF THE WORLD'S OCEANS.

THANKS FOR BEING ON THE SHOW, PROFESSOR KRAM.

THANKS FOR HAVING ME, PHIL.

Panel 2: FINALLY, HE WOULD GET THE CHANCE TO TELL THE WORLD WHAT WAS HAPPENING TO THE SEA...

PROFESSOR KRAM, AREN'T THESE PREDICTIONS RATHER EXTREME?

NOT AT ALL.

Panel 3: FIFTY YEARS AND THE OCEANS WILL ALL BE DEAD?

THAT'S NOT WHAT I SAID. MY RESEARCH SHOWS THAT IN FIFTY YEARS' TIME, OCEAN LIFE COULD BE DRASTICALLY ALTERED *IF* WE CONTINUE THE WAY WE ARE GOING.

BUT WE CAN CHANGE. IT'S NOT TOO LATE.

Panel 4: THE TV SHOW ALSO BROUGHT ON A SECOND EXPERT TO DISCUSS THE SITUATION WITH PROFESSOR KRAM.

DR. KESSEL, YOU WORK FOR GOVERNMENT FISHERY MANAGEMENT. DO YOU AGREE WITH PROFESSOR KRAM?

I DO, COMPLETELY. THAT'S WHY WE HAVE LAUNCHED A NEW FISHERY MANAGEMENT PLAN.

Panel 5: NOW, WE'RE TAKING EVEN BIGGER STEPS TOWARD PRESERVING FISH STOCKS.

BUT IT DOESN'T GO FAR ENOUGH.

Panel 6: WE *ARE* A GOVERNMENT AGENCY, AND HAVE TO TAKE POLITICAL REALITIES INTO CONSIDERATION.

WITHIN THOSE LIMITATIONS, IT'S A GOOD PLAN.

Panel 7: FIFTY YEARS, PROFESSOR KRAM? IS THAT REALLY ALL WE HAVE?

THAT'S UNKNOWABLE. WHAT WE DO KNOW IS THAT IF A NUMBER OF MAJOR SPECIES OF FISH ARE LOST, IT COULD START A CHAIN OF EVENTS THAT WILL BEGIN TO UNRAVEL THE WHOLE STRUCTURE OF LIFE IN THE OCEANS VERY QUICKLY.

DIDN'T YOU PREDICT THAT ATLANTIC HADDOCK WOULD BE GONE BY 2004?

Panel 8: NO! I SAID THAT IF THE MANAGEMENT DIDN'T CHANGE, THEY COULD DISAPPEAR BY *AS EARLY AS* 2004.

AND IT DIDN'T HAPPEN.

IT HASN'T HAPPENED *YET*. THAT'S NOT THE SAME THING.

Panel 9: UNFORTUNATELY, THAT'S ALL THE TIME WE HAVE TONIGHT. THANKS TO DR. KESSEL AND PROFESSOR KRAM FOR JOINING US THIS EVENING...

THEY'RE NOT LISTENING TO ME!

TO BE CONTINUED...

CHAPTER FOUR

BEING THE MYTH OF NATURE'S BOUNTY AND HOW SCIENTISTS GOT IT WRONG FOR MANY YEARS

But the real importance of a large number of eggs or seeds is to make up for much destruction at some period of life; and this period in the great majority of cases is an early one.

—Charles Darwin, ON THE ORIGIN OF SPECIES

SCIENTISTS AND FISHERMEN HAVE LONG DISAGREED. FISHERMEN OFTEN THINK THAT THE SCIENTISTS WHO STUDY FISH CAN'T BE BELIEVED BECAUSE THEY DON'T SPEND AS MUCH TIME AT SEA AS FISHERMEN. SCIENTISTS DON'T TRUST WHAT FISHERMEN SAY BECAUSE THEY KNOW THAT FISHERMEN HAVEN'T SPENT AS MUCH TIME IN SCHOOL AS SCIENTISTS. THE TRUTH IS: SCIENTISTS ARE SOMETIMES WRONG AND FISHERMEN ARE SOMETIMES WRONG.

IN THE 1800S, WHEN THE STUDY OF FISH and oceans was a relatively new science, it was the fishermen who were afraid that fish populations could be destroyed by catching too many fish, especially small fish. Scientists at the time believed that it was impossible to catch too many fish because fish produced so many eggs.

One of humankind's most enduring misconceptions is that of nature's bounty. That's the belief that nature is such a powerful force that it is indestructible.

Those with a religious explanation for the natural order have argued that human beings do not have the power to reverse God's creation. Even those who believe in Darwinism believe that nature is such a complex force, that there is little humans can do to interfere with it. Darwin himself never held this belief. To him, nature was about destruction and survival—and human beings were just one part of this.

Fish in particular were thought to be especially indestructible. This was because they produced enormous quantities of eggs. The fish most sought after by fishermen, codfish, were particularly abundant in eggs. A female cod that is forty inches long—not a remarkably large cod—can lay as many as three million eggs. As fish grow older and larger they produce more eggs. By the time a cod is fifty inches long, it can

ANTON VAN
LEEUWENHOEK (1632–1723)
Portrait by Jan Verkolje.

lay nine million eggs. This remarkable fact led to a great misunderstanding.

Back in the seventeenth century, Dutch scientist Anton van Leeuwenhoek, who is known as the father of microbiology, the study of the microscopic cells of which all organisms are comprised, as well as being the inventor of the microscope, attempted to count codfish eggs. He counted 9,384,000 eggs in a single, average-size fish. About 150 years later, a book called *A Cyclopedia of Commerce and Commercial Navigation* tried to verify Leeuwenhoek's findings and concluded that the egg count was "a number that will baffle all the efforts of man to exterminate." And celebrated French novelist Alexandre Dumas wrote in his spectacularly incorrect food encyclopedia, *Le Grand Dictionnaire de Cuisine,* published posthumously in 1873: "It has been calculated that if no accident prevented the hatching of the eggs and each egg reached maturity, it would take only three years to fill the sea so that you could walk across the Atlantic dryshod on the backs of cod."

The message was clear. In the late nineteenth century, a time when new technology, such as engine power, was greatly increasing fish catches, and fishermen were beginning to worry that the new modern boats were taking too many fish, scientists were telling them to catch as many fish as they could because it would be impossible to destroy fish populations.

The egg theory was refuted by Darwin himself. He pointed out that nature would have to stop overpopulation. For example, if all the cod eggs hatched and survived so that the sea was crowded with codfish, there would be too many for the food supply so that many would die off. But this would not happen because the reason nature provided fish with so many eggs is that few can survive in the sea. Those not destroyed in storms are eaten by a wide range of sea creatures, who, like humans, are fond of eating fish eggs. Mammals will usually have one to six babies. A bird will lay this many eggs, but a fish will lay millions of eggs.

ONLY RECENTLY HAS SCIENCE COME TO UNDERSTAND THAT A FISH WILL USUALLY ONLY HAVE BETWEEN ONE AND SIX SURVIVING BABIES, JUST LIKE A MAMMAL OR A BIRD.

THOMAS HENRY HUXLEY
1825–1895
An early and enthusiastic supporter of Darwin's theories, Huxley was a biologist in his own right and the first to apply Darwin's theory of evolution to human beings, an idea Darwin never explored.

One of the most influential figures promoting the idea that it was impossible for fishermen to endanger fish populations was Thomas Henry Huxley, a British scientist. Huxley greatly contributed to understanding of the anatomy of animals. He was a staunch supporter of Darwin's theories and played an important role in the public acceptance of Darwin's theory of evolution. He was also the first to suggest that birds are the modern descendants of dinosaurs, a view widely held today.

BUT ON THE SUBJECT OF FISH, HUXLEY COMPLETELY MISUNDERSTOOD DARWIN.

He believed that Darwin's theory of survival proved that fish were indestructible, concluding that commercial extinction would force fishermen to stop hunting a species long before it reached biological extinction.

Worried about the effects of technology on fish populations, the British government established a series of commissions to investigate these fears. Huxley was appointed to three of them. One of them was to examine the complaint by fishermen who caught herring in nets brought against other fishermen who caught fish on long lines of baited hooks. The herring fishermen had demanded that Parliament pass a law restricting the use of long lining. Huxley's commission rejected the claim of the herring fishermen as "unscientific." They stated that "fishermen, as a class, are exceedingly unobservant of anything about fish which is not absolutely forced upon them by their daily avocations," which established the very harmful tradition of showing contempt for the knowledge fishermen acquire through experience. What they were saying, in the end, was that fishermen know only what they need to know in order to catch fish. While this may be a little true,

THE FACT IS THAT FISHERMEN NEED TO KNOW ALMOST EVERYTHING ABOUT FISH IN ORDER TO DO A GOOD JOB OF CATCHING THEM,

and no one has a deeper involvement in or greater concern for the preservation of fish populations.

The commission also complained that the unscientific

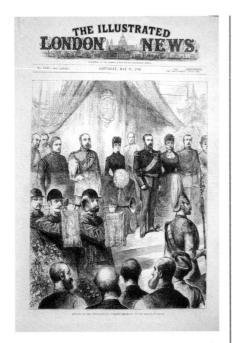

ILLUSTRATED LONDON NEWS, 1883
This front page from a British
newspaper depicts the opening of
the 1883 International Fisheries
exhibition in London; note Thomas
Henry Huxley at far left.

fishermen were interfering in "productive modes of industry." In other words, by objecting to what they saw as destructive practices, they were trying to interfere with the progress of technology. Just as computers and cyberelectronics have changed everything we do today, industry and mechanical inventions were changing the way everything was done in the late nineteenth century, an age that became known as the Industrial Revolution. Scientific, industrial, and technological progress were seen as the great path to the future. It was only in the twentieth century that we learned how such forces can also cause great damage.

Speaking at the 1883 International Fisheries Exhibition in London, which was attended by representatives of the leading fishing nations of the world, Huxley gave a speech in which he said, "Any tendency to over-fishing will meet with its natural check in the diminution of the supply. . . . In other words, we would realize we were overfishing by the simple fact that we were hauling in fewer fish." He further assured everyone that "this check will always come into operation long before anything like permanent exhaustion has occurred."

Here was science applying Darwinism to an important problem. If fishermen caused a decline in the population of fish, they could no longer fish that species because it would be too scarce, and that would allow the species to recover. But Huxley had overlooked an important part of Darwin's findings, which was that the survival struggle of

A SPECIES DEPENDED ON MAINTAINING A LARGE POPULATION.

Huxley and his commissions were extremely influential in the governments of fishing nations throughout the North Atlantic for many years to come. Later in the 1880s, when the government of Canada was considering whether their fish populations would be threatened by new fishing technologies, they quoted from Huxley and argued that despite increases in fishing, "the English fisheries show no sign of exhaustion." They concluded that "it is impossible. . . to lessen their number by the means now used for their capture."

"BY THE MEANS NOW USED FOR THEIR CAPTURE"—
HERE WAS THE HIDDEN TRAP.
MANY GOVERNMENT OFFICIALS AND SCIENTISTS
HAD FAILED TO NOTICE THAT THERE WAS
NEW TECHNOLOGY BEING USED
WITH ENTIRELY NEW RESULTS.
THEY HELD ON TO THE VIEW HUXLEY AND
OTHERS LIKE HIM SHARED LONG AFTER THE
REALITY OF THE SITUATION INDICATED
OTHERWISE. AND VERY FEW PEOPLE IN THE
WORLD TOOK NOTICE OF THE FACT THAT
HUXLEY HIMSELF,
AFTER STUDYING THE IMPACT
OF ENGINE-DRIVEN NET DRAGGERS IN
THE NORTH SEA A FEW YEARS LATER,
COMPLETELY REVERSED HIS BELIEFS.

OVERFISHING, HE ACKNOWLEDGED, WAS NOT ONLY POSSIBLE—IT WAS HAPPENING.

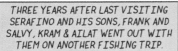

THREE YEARS AFTER LAST VISITING SERAFINO AND HIS SONS, FRANK AND SALVY, KRAM & AILAT WENT OUT WITH THEM ON ANOTHER FISHING TRIP.

NOT SO MANY BOTTOM FISH AROUND HERE THESE DAYS, BUT THE SEA IS LOADED WITH HERRING, WHICH ARE CLOSER TO THE SURFACE. WE'VE SURE GOT A LOT OF HERRING! IT'S GOOD TO HAVE SOMETHING.

. . .

SERAFINO, YOU'VE CHANGED THE BOAT COMPLETELY! WHY ARE YOU DRAGGING THE NETS SO CLOSE TO THE SURFACE NOW?

CAN YOU HEAR THAT, SERAFINO?

IT'S TOO EARLY FOR THE WHALES, KRAM.

I DON'T HEAR ANYTHING.

EXACTLY!

I THOUGHT WHALES WERE PROTECTED. NO ONE CAN HURT THEM, RIGHT?

THAT'S TRUE, AILAT. KRAM, YOU'RE MAKING YOUR DAUGHTER PARANOID, LIKE YOU.

I WASN'T TALKING ABOUT THE WHALES, SERAFINO. WHERE ARE THE BIRDS?

THERE AREN'T ANY BOTTOM FISH TO CHASE THE HERRING TO THE SURFACE ANYMORE, SO THEY WENT AWAY.

THE BIRDS WERE JUST AN ANNOYANCE, ANYWAY.

WHEN THEY RETURNED TO SHORE, AILAT, FRANK, AND SALVY WENT TO THE BEACH TO LOOK FOR CRABS . . .

I CAN'T FIND ANY!

YEAH, WE HAVEN'T SEEN ANY CRABS FOR A WHILE.

THAT EVENING, SERAFINO BROUGHT KRAM & AILAT BACK TO HIS FAVORITE RESTAURANT, CAPTAIN LEO'S, FOR DINNER.

I CAN'T WAIT TO EAT A BIG HALIBUT STEAK!

HA HA!

CAPTAIN LEO'S

I'M SORRY, WE HAVEN'T HAD ANY HALIBUT IN QUITE SOME TIME. HOWEVER, WE HAVE GRILLED HERRING, POACHED HERRING, AND BLACKENED HERRING.

WHAT CAN I GET FOR YOU INSTEAD?

UM . . .

TO BE CONTINUED . . .

CHAPTER FIVE

BEING A CONCISE HISTORY OF THE POLITICS OF FISH

Rarity . . . is the precursor to extinction.

—Charles Darwin, ON THE ORIGIN OF SPECIES

THE ARGUMENT ABOUT OVERFISHING ENDED IN THE 1990S ON THE GRAND BANKS. THESE SHALLOW STRETCHES OF SEA OFF OF THE ATLANTIC COAST WERE THE MOST CELEBRATED FISHING GROUNDS IN THE WORLD. FOR CENTURIES, FISHERMEN CAME FROM EUROPE AND ASIA TO FISH THE GRAND BANKS.

BUT IN THE SECOND HALF OF THE twentieth century, fishermen noticed two things:

1. THEY HAD TO TRAVEL GREATER DISTANCES TO FIND THE SAME AMOUNT OF FISH THEY USED TO FIND CLOSE TO SHORE.

2. THE FISH WERE GETTING SMALLER.

As a fish population gets smaller, nature tends to help the species by allowing the fish to produce young at an earlier age. But since the big fish that produce the most eggs are also the easiest to catch, they get taken first, leaving a population of small fish behind. Nature also compensates for a shortage of food by making fish grow more slowly.

Once again, it was the fishermen and not the scientists who were expressing the most concern about the size of the fish and the distances needed to travel in order to catch them. The only problem was that most fishermen thought of overfishing as something that was done by fishermen in other countries. Even today, most fishermen in the world, no matter where they live, will say that the worst fishing practices are those done by foreigners.

An interview with an English fishing boat captain from the Cornish port of Newlyn illustrates that point. In 1995, that fishing boat captain, William Hooper, was asked about the problem of overfishing. He talked about how when he started fishing in 1955, the catches would be so high on the deck the fish would be up to his knees. He said that as the catches got smaller, he was forced to get bigger and more powerful boats just to catch the same amount of fish. He had started with a forty-foot boat and now had a much-better-equipped fifty-five-foot boat that was not bringing in as many fish as he caught on the small boat in 1955.

Hooper was very clear on the cause of his problem: it was overfishing.

BUT WHAT OR WHO WAS CAUSING THIS OVERFISHING?

His answer was clear: "The biggest problem we have is the Spanish." Only a few months before, the European government had given permission for Spanish fishermen to fish in his waters. When it was pointed out to Hooper that only forty boats had been allowed in the waters and they were just now arriving, which meant they couldn't have been responsible for the overfishing in his waters, he thought in silence for a minute and then said: "Yes, the Scots used to overfish."

THE MOVEMENT TO THROW foreigners off of native fishing grounds reached its height on the island nation of Iceland. This may be because there were rational reasons to think foreigners were the problem in Iceland. Iceland is far enough away from other countries, without anyone on their borders, so Icelanders feel alone in

This map of Europe shows how distant Iceland is from the mainland. The closest country in Europe is Norway, which is more than 600 miles away.

the world. For centuries, the island was a neglected colony of Denmark, with little money spent to develop it. Iceland was far poorer than North America or northern Europe, and Icelanders fished in small wooden open-deck boats powered by rows of men with oars—a boat not very different from those used by their Viking ancestors. They would drag them into the sea in the cold, early morning from the lava-encrusted beaches.

In the 1890s, however, modern, steel-hulled, engine-powered fishing boats from England started dragging their enormous nets through Icelandic waters. These were some of the fishing boats that were fleeing the overfished North Sea fishing grounds, a fact that should have been seen as a warning to Icelanders.

And to many it was. But there was a debate in Iceland between those who thought these boats should be kept out of their waters and those who thought Iceland should get a few of their own. This debate intensified after 1944 when Iceland became independent. In their plan to develop their economy, fishing was given the most important place. A national economy based on the danger and uncertainty of commercial fishing was a common idea in earlier centuries, but by the twentieth century this was unusual. But Iceland is an unusual place: an island of volcanoes and glaciers in a harsh climate where neither trees nor grains will grow, and children took a small piece of dried cod to school for a snack because there was no bread for sandwiches.

ONE OF THEIR FEW NATURAL RESOURCES WAS THEIR SEA FULL OF FISH, AND THEY COULD NOT RISK LOSING THEIR MAIN FOOD SUPPLY.

And so they asked the foreign fisher-men to leave. In international law, the sea is not treated the same as the land, and own-ership of the sea was not widely accepted. Some regarded it as an act of war to bar ships from the sea. The British, although they were trying to do the same thing to other Europe-ans in their own waters, claimed that hav-ing their fishing boats banned from Icelandic waters was an act of war. The British Royal Navy attacked the Icelandic Coast Guard, which protected their water. The Coast Guard was the only military Iceland had. Between 1958 and 1975, the British Navy and the Icelandic Coast guard fought three nearly bloodless but nevertheless vio-lent and dangerous wars on the high seas around Iceland. Few shots were fired, but nets were cut and ships were rammed. At the end, Iceland established a zone of 200 miles around Icelandic territories in which only Icelanders could fish. They had gained control of their fishing grounds and they carefully regulated it to maintain their fish populations.

But once the Icelanders had their 200-mile limit, the other nations of the world wanted theirs. Countries began mea-suring 200 miles from every farthest rock they could claim.

BRITISH TRAWLER *COVENTRY CITY* FACES OFF AGAINST ICELANDIC COAST GUARD VESSEL *ALBERT* OFF THE WESTFJORDS IN 1958
A camera caught this confrontation between these vessels during the first Cod War, which ended in an accord that any future disagreements between the two nations would be arbitrated by the International Court of Justice in The Hague.

WITH GLOBAL WARMING, THE SEAS ARE RISING

and some of these rocks may become submerged, costing nations large expanses of exclusive fishing grounds. Most of the proven fishing grounds of the planet are now under the exclusive control of a single nation or group of nations.

Most countries, once they gained control of their fishing grounds, increased their fishing. In the late 1970s, many governments invested money in building up fishing fleets. Both fishermen and governments reasoned that because they had removed the cause of overfishing—foreigners—they were now free to catch more fish. They built larger boats with better equipment.

At first, many more fish were caught and more money was made. But in time, the 200-mile limit was a disaster.

SOME GOVERNMENTS, LIKE THE UNITED STATES, made money available for fishermen to buy new boats. Others, such as Canada, built fishing fleets themselves. For a time, it worked well for Canada—especially Newfoundland and Labrador, a poor province that survived almost entirely on fishing for cod. Fishermen, fish companies, and the Canadian government were all making money. Fish, an important export for Canada, was helping the country to bring in money from other countries. Thanks to the new 200-mile limit, almost everyone in Atlantic Canada was happy for more than ten years.

But there was one unhappy group: a group of fishermen in Newfoundland. These were tough and hearty men who lived in little villages along the coast and went to sea the way their grandfathers and great-grandfathers had, in small wooden boats called skiffs. They dropped traps made of knotted rope and left them there until they filled with cod and were ready to haul up. Or they fished with a baited hook on a line that they hauled up by hand. It was dangerous work in icy waters full of treacherous icebergs that had broken off from the polar cap. The water was so cold that they would freeze to death in minutes if they fell in. When their catches got smaller and smaller, they thought it was because the big, new boats far out at sea were taking all the fish. At that point, it was only their inshore fish that were vanishing, so the deepwater fishermen paid little attention. Even in the 1980s, a century after trawlers were found to be destroying the North Sea, many still believed that the codfish population of the Grand Banks,

known as the northern stock, was in no danger because it was one of the most plentiful fish populations in recorded history.

THE SKIFF FISHERMEN WENT TO SCIENTISTS, AND MANY SCIENTISTS AGREED WITH THEM. BUT THE GOVERNMENT HAD THEIR OWN SCIENTISTS WHO REPORTED THAT THE NORTHERN STOCK WAS NOT IN DANGER.

So many fish were being caught and so much money was being made that the government didn't want to listen to a few old-fashioned skiff fishermen. They were providing jobs processing fish at sea for many people who had not had any work before the 200-mile limit. The Canadian fleet was landing huge quantities of cod, more than ever before, so there had to be a lot of fish out there.

For centuries, cod fishermen in Newfoundland braved the icy waters of the Grand Banks in dories (small boats with high sides and flat bottoms) that offered little protection against the raging sea.

BUT THEY DIDN'T CONSIDER THE OTHER POSSIBILITY: THAT THE CATCHES WERE LARGE BECAUSE THEY WERE CATCHING ALL OF THE FISH.

Ralph Mayo, a marine biologist in New England, compared the problem of measuring fish populations to measuring icebergs. It is generally agreed only 10 percent of an iceberg is actually visible above the ocean: the other 90 percent is hidden under the ocean. Mayo called this the "perception problem." With fish, he said, you "see some cod and assume this is the tip of the iceberg. But it could be the whole iceberg."

And in the case of the cod, it turned out to be the entire iceberg. What happened on the Grand Banks is that modern fishing had become so powerful, so effective, the fishermen were able to hunt down every last fish in a dying population without realizing that it was dying. In the case of the codfish on the Grand Banks, the catches were quite large until suddenly,

THERE WERE NO MORE FISH.

So in 1992, John Crosbie, the Canadian Fishing Minister, announced that the northern stock had nearly vanished. No one would be allowed to fish cod in the Grand Banks until the population was replenished. Thirty thousand Newfoundland fishermen instantly lost their jobs. The island province was plunged into poverty.

In 1994, the ban was extended to almost all the fishing grounds in the area. These were seen as temporary measures, but more than fifteen years later, the cod population has shown no sign of recovery, and it seems the people of Newfoundland will not be getting back their livelihoods. There are still cod there, but the population has not regenerated. Perhaps the cod had lost its place in the food chain and other animals were now eating its food. Perhaps, as Darwin had suggested, the population had become too few to sustain the species—rarity, Darwin had stated clearly, leads to extinction.

But at least the fundamental debate was now over. There could be no denying that overfishing was a real threat, that huge populations, even the most numerous, could be permanently destroyed by the unrestrained acts of humans. Now the debate shifted from the question of whether overfishing was leading to the decline of fish in the ocean to what should be done to prevent this from happening.

ON AILAT'S 14TH BIRTHDAY, KRAM TOOK HER BACK TO THE CARIBBEAN TO GO SNORKELING AGAIN.

THE BEACHFRONT HOTEL WHERE THEY ONCE STAYED HAD SINCE FALLEN INTO DISREPAIR, AS THOUGH IT HAD NOT BEEN CARED FOR IN YEARS.

WOW, AILAT. THIS PLACE HAS REALLY CHANGED!

AS THEY WALKED TO THE BEACH, THEY NOTICED HOW FEW PEOPLE WERE IN THE WATER.

LOOK, DAD. THERE ARE NO MORE FISHERMEN ON THE BEACH ANYMORE.

THAT'S NOT GOOD.

THE WATER HAD BECOME GREEN AND SLIMY.

GROSS! WHAT IS THIS STUFF?

IT'S ALGAE.

YUCK!

THINGS WERE VERY DIFFERENT UNDERWATER, TOO. PARTS OF THE REEF WERE STILL ALIVE, BUT MOST OF IT WAS BROWN AND DEAD, COVERED IN ALGAE. ALL THE BRIGHTLY COLORED FISH THEY HAD SEEN ON THEIR LAST TRIP WERE NOW GONE.

WHEN THEY SURFACED, AILAT BEGAN TO CRY...

WHAT HAPPENED, DAD? DID THEY TAKE TOO MANY PARROT FISH?

WELL, THAT DIDN'T HELP, BUT...

KRAM EXPLAINED THAT THE HOTEL WAS BUILT TOO CLOSE TO THE SHORE, CAUSING MUDSLIDES AND BLOCKING OUT THE SUN, WHICH CHOKED THE REEF TO DEATH.

THAT HOTEL IS THE MAIN PROBLEM

DAD, I WANT TO GO HOME, NOW.

ME, TOO, AILAT. ME, TOO.

TO BE CONTINUED...

CHAPTER SIX

BEING AN EXAMINATION OF WHY WE CAN'T SIMPLY STOP FISHING

. . . mitigate the destruction ever so little, and the number of species will almost instantaneously increase to any amount.

—Charles Darwin, ON THE ORIGIN OF SPECIES

It would seem that the simplest and surest solution to helping fish repopulate the oceans would be to just stop all fishing. After all, a complete end to fishing would remove a constant and important predator from the food chain.

But while it might save the fish in the short term, we can't predict what the environmental impact of suddenly removing a major predator from the ocean would do to the earth's natural order.

WHAT'S MORE, FISH HAVE BEEN A STAPLE of the human diet for hundreds of thousands of years. It is an extremely healthy source of protein, and fish, especially the mid-water varieties, are often prescribed by cardiologists to patients with heart disease. And lastly, of course, completely eliminating fishing would destroy peoples' lives.

To see this requires only a glimpse at modern Newfoundland. After the codfish ban in the 1990s, Newfoundland lost its way of life. Not only were the fishermen put out of work, so were the people who processed fish, and the people who marketed fish, and the people who transported fish. Most of the population, in fact, was out of work, supported solely by the money handed out from the Canadian government to help them.

The cod never returned to Newfoundland and life changed. Where there had been cod, there was now crab. The fishermen were not certain if these crab had moved in because of the absence of the predator, cod, or if they had simply always been there but no one had cared until the cod was gone.

Inshore fishermen who had been getting eighteen and a half cents a pound for cod were now getting a dollar and sixty cents Canadian for crab. Gone were the thirty-foot open-deck skiffs from which the inshore fishermen trapped cod. Now the inshore fishermen drag up their skiffs to lie in the weeds, and buy bigger boats to go farther out and set baited traps. The offshore fishermen started crabbing, too. The draggers removed the huge spools of net from their sterns and hauled in crab traps on pulleys fixed on the sides of the boats. The fish-processing plants were now all crab-processing plants. But it was a short season—about two months in the summer, and only 25,000 pounds of crab were allowed for each license.

Along with the environmental loss, Newfoundland lost its culture. Human beings are part of the natural order, so it's not surprising to find human society follows the same natural laws as biology. Just as species need diversity in order to survive and prosper, it may be that human civilization needs a wide variety of cultures, different ways of life, in order to survive and prosper. We live in a world in which cultures and ways of life are vanishing at an enormous rate. In the United States alone, thousands of family farms are closed down every year, changing the relationship of people to the land, the nature of rural life, and the kind of food we eat. Online shopping is threatening the culture of shopkeepers. The world is losing many of its languages. Only eighty-three out of 7,000 languages are commonly spoken today, and linguists estimate that a language from somewhere on earth dies as frequently as every other week.

MANY THINGS, NOT JUST FISH, ARE IN DANGER OF EXTINCTION. FISHERMEN ARE IN DANGER OF EXTINCTION.

As with animal species, whenever anything is threatened with extinction, it is worthwhile to ask what will take its place. In the case of fishermen, it appears to be tourism.

In Newfoundland, that's already happened. The grocery stores and little shops in just about every little fishing village have started selling souvenirs to visitors. What kind of souvenirs? Cod. Cod hats, cod T-shirts, cod-shaped chocolates, cod-shaped cookies, cod ornaments and sculptures and business-card holders. One line of cod cookies was labeled "endangered species." In the ultimate irony, the restaurants that cater to tourists import cod for their menus because when people travel to Newfoundland, they want to eat cod.

When the parks department of Canada proposed turning Bonavista Bay, a one-time inshore fishing ground, into an aquatic reserve for tourists, the fishermen rebelled. This is one of fishermen's most dreaded scenarios—that their boats will end up in museums and their fishing grounds will be used only for viewing sea life, like the great African plains where tourists go to view animals. The Bonavista Bay fishermen MOUNTED SUCH A VOCIFEROUS OPPOSITION TO THIS PLAN FOR THEIR FUTURE THAT THE PROJECT WAS DROPPED.

THIS TENSION BETWEEN THE TOURISM and fishing industries, really a struggle for the character and culture of coastlines, can be seen along many of the seasides of the world.

Fishing has always attracted people. Many of the most famous fishing ports have drawn artists and writers. One of the most important movements in modern art, fauvism, began in May of 1905 when French painters Henri Matisse and André Derain went to the Mediterranean anchovy port of

THE HARBOR AT COLLIOURE
The brightly painted fishing boats in the port city of Collioure in southwest
France inspired artists Henri Matisse and André Derain to use bold colors and
broad brushwork in their paintings, which sparked a movement that became
known as fauvism.

Collioure and painted the colorful fishing boats in pure, bright colors. Rudyard Kipling's famous book, *Captains Courageous*, is about a boy who accidentally serves on a Gloucester schooner to the Grand Banks, and the American classic *Moby Dick* by Herman Melville starts in the New Bedford and Nantucket whale fisheries.

Fishing has always been at the heart of the culture of nations with coastlines.

And at first glance, it would seem that tourism and fishing could coexist well. Tourists, like artists, love working fishing towns. But in the conflict between the interests of tourism and fishing, waterfront space becomes a vital issue. Yacht owners pay prices fishermen can't afford for harbor-front mooring and dock space. In the end, they compete for almost everything.

A WORLD WITHOUT FISHING WOULD BE SAD.

Coastlines would lose their meaning and coastal people would lose their culture and their primary way of earning money. It was a way of life for thousands of years without destroying the environment. And so governments, fishermen, and scientists need to work together to find a way to fish without destroying the fish.

The goal is to find ways in which fishing can continue while still maintaining large fish populations where many fish are allowed to grow to be very large. If this formula can be found, if the fish populations can reproduce enough so that the new fish make up for the amount of fish taken by fishermen, fishing can continue forever.

THIS IS CALLED SUSTAINABLE FISHING.

THIS IS THE REAL ANSWER TO OVERFISHING.

The question is: How is sustainable fishing done? For thousands of years, fishing was sustainable. But nowadays, between 100 and 120 million tons of sea life are killed by fishing every year. We have seen that life in the ocean can't reproduce fast enough every year to make up for the loss. So something must be done.

THE STORY OF KRAM AND AILAT : PART 7

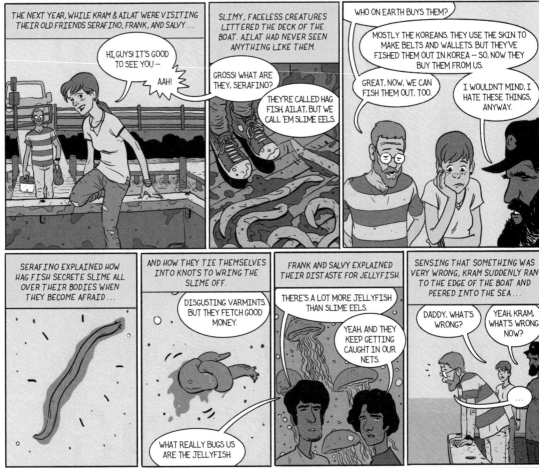

CHAPTER SEVEN

BEING A DETAILED LOOK AT FOUR POSSIBLE SOLUTIONS AND WHY THEY ALONE WON'T WORK

From the continued preservation of the individuals best fitted

for the two sites, two varieties might slowly be formed.

These varieties would cross and blend where they met.

—Charles Darwin, ON THE ORIGIN OF SPECIES

FARMING FISH IS SOMETIMES THOUGHT OF AS A SOLUTION.

JUST AS DOMESTIC ANIMALS ARE FARMED TO PROVIDE MOST OF THE WORLD'S MEAT WITHOUT DEPLETING THE WILD MAMMAL POPULATION, MIGHT NOT SOMETHING SIMILAR BE DONE WITH FISH?

IF CERTAIN FISH POPULATIONS could be raised like cattle, wouldn't that save the wild species? The idea of fish farming, which is taking fish from the wild and keeping them in ponds so that they reproduce and provide a constant source of fish, is not new. The Chinese did this with carp, a freshwater fish, 4,500 years ago, feeding them the leftovers from the worm cultivation of their silk industry. There is also evidence of such fish ponds with the ancient Hebrews and ancient Egyptians. The Romans learned to cultivate both fish and oysters.

In some ways, the idea of fish farming seems like a good one. But upon closer examination, supplying people with farmed fish doesn't actually save wild fish at sea. Most farmed fish are fed wild fish that are caught by net draggers the size of factories. These ships indiscriminately scoop up fish by the thousands and grind them up into fish meal, which is then pressed into fish pellets to feed to the fish back on the farm. In the case of salmon, it has been estimated that four pounds of wild fish are fed to grow one pound of farmed fish.

There is also that old problem of Darwin and evolution. Animals adapt to their environment, and change. We have already seen this in the farming and domestication of mammals. A dog only vaguely resembles a wolf. A cow barely

AUROCH
(*Bos primigenius*)

An ancestor of domestic cattle, aurochs inhabited Europe, Asia, and North Africa until they became extinct in 1627.

resembles an auroch, the swift-footed, ferocious animal from which it is descended (aurochs were hunted into extinction about four hundred years ago).

The fact that farmed fish are considerably different from their wild ancestors is immediately apparent. Because they live in overcrowded pens and swim much less than their wild cousins, the muscle tissue of farmed fish have a different consistency. Some species don't even look like their wild ancestors anymore. A farmed striped bass resembles a wild one only in the black and silver stripes for which it was named. The farmed striped bass are much smaller and have an entirely different shape to their pointy heads and short bodies.

But a greater problem in farm fishing is that farmed fish lose their survival skills. A fish pen does not have the survival struggle of the wild. There are no predators there and fish are largely protected from storms and temperature changes.

PUT BACK INTO THE WILD, A FARMED FISH WOULD PROBABLY NOT KNOW HOW TO SURVIVE.

If a farmed fish mated with a wild fish, their offspring might also lack these survival skills. A salmon might not know to return up the river of its birth for spawning. A cod might lack the enzyme that it needs to release to keep from freezing in subarctic water. Even just a few farm fish accidentally released into the wild could menace the survival of an entire wild population.

Furthermore, overcrowded pens produce such enormous quantities of waste—including chemicals that are sometimes used—that they pollute surrounding waters. While the fish-farming industry is well aware of these problems and is trying to address them with such ideas as vegetable alternatives to feed, such measures will take the farmed species even further away from the wild species and make them even more dangerous for the evolution of the species.

It should also be remembered that while the problem is preserving fish, fish farming does nothing to preserve fisheries.

SO IF FISH FARMING ISN'T A GOOD solution, what about limiting the fish that fishermen are allowed to catch?

It seems obvious that if the problem is that fishermen are catching too many fish, the solution should be to tell them to catch less. That has been done. But it is not a simple solution.

FISHERMEN CANNOT BE TOLD SIMPLY TO CATCH FEWER FISH.

A SYSTEM OF RULES HAS TO BE ESTABLISHED THAT CAN BE ENFORCED WITH PENALTIES

for those found catching more than they are allowed. The number must be established for each species in each fishing area and it has to change regularly because fish populations change. What is the total population in the area for each species? Since the fish cannot be seen and they move around, they are difficult to count. Scientists test small parts of the ocean by fishing with nets and then using a computer to estimate the total population based on that catch. But they make mistakes. Sometimes they allow too many fish to be caught because they thought the population was bigger than it actually was. Iceland, after successfully estimating their cod population for decades, overcalculated for a few years and allowed fishermen to take too many cod from their fishing grounds. This led to a major crisis in the Icelandic fishery, which had been considered one of the best managed fisheries in the world.

The estimates have to be taken constantly, and must take into account shifts in the weather, changes in the population of the fish, mammals and birds that feed on the fish, and even changes in their food supply.

THE SECOND PROBLEM WITH REGULATING IN THIS WAY, WHICH IS KNOWN AS FISHING QUOTAS, IS THAT MOST FISH THAT ARE CAUGHT ARE DEAD by the time they reach the fisherman's deck. If the fisherman has caught more fish than he is allowed, he must take some of these dead fish and throw them overboard. Fishermen hate wasting fish like this, and yet millions of pounds of FISH ARE THROWN OVERBOARD EVERY YEAR BECAUSE OF THESE LAWS.

These laws also give fishermen an incentive to waste fish. A fisherman hauls in his net, calls into the markets on his cell phone to find out what fish are selling for the highest price that day, and then dumps the fish that is selling for the lowest prices. Why would he use up his quota on a species on a day when the price is low?

Another problem is that the quota system tends to direct fishermen to constantly target new species. This happened in New England. When the cod quota was small, fishermen went after haddock, which are in the same biological family as cod. Darwin noted that competition is particularly intense between related species because they tend to eat similar things. Because fishermen interfered with these struggles by killing large numbers of cod, the haddock population flourished. Great cod ports, such as Gloucester, have become haddock ports now. But if the fishermen also kill too many of the haddock before the cod have recovered, a wide swath out of the food chain will have been irreparably damaged, shifting the entire balance of nature.

THERE IS ALSO THE ISSUE OF BY-CATCH.

Dragging nets is not a perfect science and although fishermen adjust the depth of the net and other factors to pursue a particular species, there are always a few other species that turn up in the net. This is the by-catch. The number of species of by-catch commonly hauled in vary depending on the diversity of the fishing grounds. In some places, a well-targeted drag may bring in only one or two other types of fish. Off of Cornwall, where a number of ocean systems meet on the southwestern tip of England, it is common to haul in twenty different species.

SHRIMP TRAWLER BY-CATCH
Scientists estimate that for every pound of shrimp caught, there may be up to twelve times that in wasteful by-catch.

By-catch is a dilemma for regulators because fishermen cannot avoid it and it would be extremely wasteful to
throw out all the accidentally caught fish. In New England,
the approach has generally been to permit by-catch. A fisherman targeting flounder is permitted to land whatever cod
turn up in the net. When the by-catch starts getting larger
than the target species, though, questions have to be asked
about which is really the target. In 2007, the United States
started putting a quota on the amount of by-catch allowed.

In 2007, the British government, after what they said
was a five-year investigation, charged seventeen fishermen
and ship owners from the port of Newlyn in Cornwall with
illegally landing fish that were over quota. Unwilling to
throw away valuable fish that were already dead but were
over quota, six Newlyn vessels had been landing more than
their quota of cod, hake, and monkfish by mislabeling them
as ling, turbot, and bass—fish for which there were no quotas.
The fact that it took five years to catch them may indicate
how little regulators know about fish.

The Cornish fishermen did not deny their crime, but
argued that while barely eeking out a living, they could not
bring themselves to throw out valuable fish that were dead
anyway. One of the accused, Steve Hicks, a former police-

man, told the London *Guardian*, "We knew we were doing wrong. But it wasn't done with greed. It was done to make a living." A British government spokesman called the case "a major success in the control of overfishing," which is probably true from an administrative point of view. From a biological one, this seems less certain. Drew Davies, another one of the fishing boat captains, said that during one trip

HE HAD BEEN FORCED TO DUMP A THOUSAND DEAD COD OVERBOARD. "THERE IS NOTHING WORSE FOR A FISHERMAN THAN DOING THAT," HE SAID.

AN ALTERNATIVE TO QUOTAS, or limiting the amount of fish a fisherman can catch, would be to limit the amount of time he is allowed to fish. This has ended up being a particularly harsh measure for most fishermen in the United States because not only are they limited in the number of days in the year they can fish (many of them are allowed less than fifty days a year), but because of the quotas, they are also limited in how much they can catch when they do go out.

IT IS EXTREMELY DESTRUCTIVE TO A FISHING SOCIETY TO STOP FISHERMEN FROM WORKING.

It is destructive to any society to bar people from their work. A fisherman is, by nature, a hard worker, and being told he can only work two months out of every year is unbearable to him. Also, fishing boats are expensive to maintain, and fifty days of fishing might not earn enough money even to pay for keeping the boat in good shape.

The number of days allowed varies depending on factors, such as gear type. Because the days at sea were determined as a percentage of the days a vessel had been fishing when the regulation was first imposed, it favors the most destructive kind of fishing, the large, bottom draggers. Since these vessels could stay out at sea for weeks and every fifteen hours was counted as a day, they got the most days at sea.

Limits on days, along with high fuel prices, make fishermen want to stay close to home when fishing instead of using up precious fishing days—not to mention fuel—traveling to and from distant fishing waters. The problem with this is that whenever fishing is concentrated on one area, it has an enormous negative impact on that area.

Fishermen have tried to find ways to get around the time-limit regulations. Many have bought several boats, or gone into partnership with several boat owners so that once a vessel uses up its allotted days, the fishermen can simply take out another vessel for a few months. This is what was happening in Iceland until the government discontinued days-at-sea limits, finding it wasteful to encourage fishermen to have this huge fleet of boats sitting underutilized in their harbors.

Other fishermen have turned to gill netting. This is an old fishing technique in which a net is anchored in the sea. Fish swim into the net and get caught in the holes in the mesh, literally grabbed in the gills by the net. The advantage of this is that a fisherman can leave the net at sea and come back for it later, so the fisherman is not using up his days-at-sea time or fuel.

But there is an environmental problem with gill nets. They are wasteful. The nets catch fish indiscriminately, and SOMETIMES THEY BREAK AWAY FROM THEIR MOORINGS AND ROAM THE OCEAN, CONTINUING TO CATCH FISH UNTIL THE NET IS SO FISH-LADEN IT SINKS TO THE BOTTOM OF THE OCEAN TO BECOME FOOD FOR PREDATORS.

In New England, fishermen have started experiment-ing with self-regulation. A group of fishermen form a sector and agree that this group will fish only a specific quantity of each of the seventeen species of groundfish that are allowed in New England. The group regulates themselves however they want, as long as at the end of a year they have landed only the prescribed quantity. These fishing sectors have been able to meet these goals without limiting days at sea or the amount of catch on a trip, so there is no need to throw fish overboard. The experiment seems to support the long-held view that fishermen can regulate a fishery better than government can. But they are closely monitored.

ANOTHER POSSIBILITY THAT HAS HAD SOME success in recent years in both the Atlantic and the Pacific is temporarily closing off certain areas from fishing. Then, after a few years when the fish in that area appear to have recovered from the damage of fishing, the area can be opened up again—and then a different area can be closed off. Such a system depends on defining more than two grounds. It does no good to close off an area only to send all the fishermen to destroy a second area. But if there are a number of areas used in rotation, extensive damage to any single area may be avoided.

We know that fish populations will sometimes recover if left alone. The greatest catches in modern European history were after World War II because warfare had made it too dangerous to fish for five years. During that period, the fish populations became enormous in the North Atlantic, leading Europeans to often joke that a world war is an effective way to regulate a fishery.

BUT, OF COURSE, A WAR ISN'T NECESSARY. IT WAS THE FIVE YEARS WITHOUT FISHING THAT WAS EFFECTIVE.

When Europeans first started fishing in North America, they were amazed at the size of the fish populations. One Italian account of Newfoundland in 1497 reported that the fish were so thick that a fisherman didn't even need a net to haul them in, but could simply lower a weighted basket and scoop them up. In 1602, a man named Bartholomew Gosnold, on a voyage to America in search of sassafras plants, a valued medicine at the time, gave Cape Cod its name when he complained that his boat was constantly "pestered" by thick schools of codfish as he tried to get around the peninsula.

The reason the pre-European American waters had so many fish was that the native Americans living there, unlike Europeans, didn't engage in large-scale commercial fishing. They only fished for their dinners.

WHEN FISHING AREAS ARE CLOSED OFF FOR A NUMBER OF YEARS, THEY USUALLY RECOVER. BUT IT IS HARD TO KNOW HOW LONG YOU HAVE TO WAIT.

And if too much destruction has been allowed, they may never recover, which is what seems to be the case in the Canadian Grand Banks.

This type of regulating holds great promise, though. Unfortunately, it's based on human calculations: how to define the fishing areas that need to be closed off, when to close them, which ones to close off first, and when to open them again. These are very difficult decisions. For all the successes with this type of regulation, there have also been failures. And the real problem is that we have driven nature so far, so fast, that we simply cannot afford to make any more mistakes.

One of the greatest problems in fishery management is this species-by-species approach. If cod stocks are down and herring stocks are up, these are not unrelated problems, because cod feed on herring. But there is no one in charge of managing the ecosystem. The fact that everything that happens in nature affects everything else is forgotten in the bureaucracy of fishery management. Large holes can develop in the ecosystem without anyone noticing. Scientists suddenly realized that many sharks were vanishing from the Gulf of Mexico, and that the barndoor skate, a large raylike predator, was vanishing from New England. But no one had been watching because no fishery targeted these noncommercial species. They were being killed in by-catches.

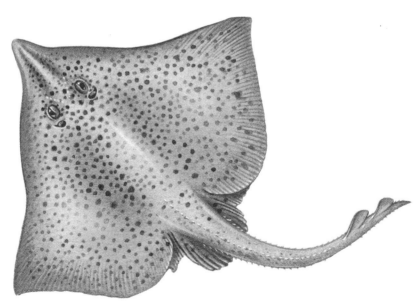

BARNDOOR SKATE
(*Dipturus laevis*)
One of the largest skates found in the North Atlantic, the population of the barndoor skate has dramatically declined in the last fifty years primarily through by-catch due to intensive trawling. It is now listed as endangered by the World Conservation Union.

DANIEL PAULY, A SCIENTIST AT THE UNIVERSITY OF BRITISH COLUMBIA AND ONE OF THE LEADING EXPERTS ON FISH-STOCK ASSESSMENT, IS ONE OF THE MANY SCIENTISTS WHO HAS CALLED FOR "ECOSYSTEM-BASED MANAGEMENT" BUT THE IDEA IS ONLY CATCHING ON VERY SLOWLY. THE BUREAUCRACY NEEDS TO READ DARWIN.

SEVERAL YEARS LATER, KRAM AND AILAT WERE AT THE BEACH, DISCUSSING THE SEA TURNING ORANGE.

IT'S LIKE THIS EVERYWHERE, NOW.

AILAT REACHED DOWN TO TOUCH THE OCEAN WATER.

IT FEELS SLIPPERY, LIKE THOSE SLIME EELS.

IT'S NOT FROM THE SLIME EELS, SARDINE. IT'S FROM THE BILLIONS OF PLANKTON WITHOUT ANIMALS TO EAT IT.

PLANKTON IS ORANGE, BUT IN SOME PLACES, IT LOOKS MORE PINKISH.

THERE'S NO ONE ON THE BEACH ANYMORE.

YEAH. NO CRABS, EITHER. AND NO BIRDS.

I CAN'T SAY THAT I BLAME THEM.

I TRIED TO WARN PEOPLE. DID I SAY IT IN THE WRONG WAY?

CHEER UP, DAD. LET'S GO AND VISIT SERAFINO.

THEY FOUND SERAFINO SITTING ON HIS FRONT PORCH.

I'M THROUGH WITH FISHING. FRANK AND SALVY ARE STILL AT IT, THOUGH.

I DON'T UNDER-STAND HOW THIS HAPPENED.

LATER, KRAM AND AILAT SPENT THE AFTERNOON WITH FRANK AND SALVY, WHO SHOWED THEM HOW THEY FISH FOR KRILL.

SEE THESE LITTLE SHRIMP? THEY'RE KRILL! THE OCEAN IS FULL OF 'EM!

BUT DON'T WHALES EAT KRILL?

YEAH, AND IT'S GOOD STUFF!

WHAT WILL THE WHALES EAT???

RELAX, GUYS. THERE'S ENOUGH TO GO AROUND. THE SEALS DIED OFF BECAUSE THEY LIVED ON FISH -- BUT THERE IS PLENTY OF KRILL LEFT FOR THE WHALES.

IT WON'T LAST IF YOU KEEP TAKING IT, THOUGH!

AW, AILAT, YOU SOUND JUST LIKE YOUR DAD.

HA HA HA HA

LATER THAT NIGHT, AT CAPTAIN LEO'S ...

TONIGHT'S SPECIAL IS A REAL TREAT, KRILL SALAD!

TO BE CONTINUED ...

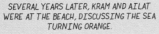

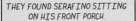
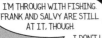

CHAPTER EIGHT

THE BEST SOLUTION TO OVERFISHING: SUSTAINABLE FISHING

There is grandeur in this view of life . . . from so simple a beginning endless forms most beautiful have been, and are being evolved.

—Charles Darwin, ON THE ORIGIN OF SPECIES

So many of the problems of modern fishing were created by the development of equipment that was just

TOO EFFICIENT.

The problem is that

TECHNOLOGY, ONCE

it is invented, is very difficult to suppress.

IF IT WORKS WELL, PEOPLE WANT IT.

THERE HAVE BEEN MANY STUDIES on the harmful effects of cars, for instance, but it isn't likely that any society will be persuaded to ban them. What we have done is to ban certain types of cars and certain types of automobile technology, although many argue that this has not gone far enough.

Limits on fishing technology have been accepted for a very long time. As far back as the Middle Ages, when fishing communities first recognized that nets would destroy fish populations if they caught too many young fish, they increased the size of the open spaces in their nets, making it possible for the smallest fish to escape. In a modern dragger, this doesn't work because so many fish are scooped up that the smaller ones aren't even able to get to the back of the net to escape. The struggle was perfectly illustrated in the animated film *Finding Nemo.*

Many of the regulations on fishing gear have been aimed at the most destructive type of fishing vessel: the bottom dragger. History shows that since it was invented, wherever this type of ship has gone it has left the fish populations depleted. When bottom draggers were first introduced to New England in the early twentieth century, the *Gloucester Daily Times* warned that if they were not banned in their infancy they would become too powerful, too central a feature of the fishing fleets to ever be completely banned. This has happened. There have been attempts to restrict the size of the vessel, the engine power, and even the size of the net. In many places, rock hoppers have been banned. But suggestions that bottom draggers themselves be banned are usually met with outrage or disbelief by most fishermen. They argue that banning bottom dragging would only lead to other destructive forms of fishing. Besides, they suggest, if the idea is to ban destructive technologies, then one could argue that banning the use of engines is a good idea. After all, from the perspective of history, it seems clear that the large-scale destruction of the ocean's fish began with the use of engines. Shouldn't we go back to sail power?

THIS WOULD BE LIKE SUGGESTING THAT EVERYONE STOP USING CARS AND RIDE ON HORSEBACK INSTEAD.

The issue of safety is also a concern. Even today, fishing is still considered to be the most dangerous job in the world. It has the highest percentage of death and injury—more than even firefighters or police officers. A statue in Gloucester lists the names of more than five thousand local fishermen who have been lost at sea since 1623, though historians think there may be as many as five thousand more whose names have been lost. One or two more names are added to the list every year, usually in the winter. But in the days of sail power, dozens of ships with hundreds of men could be lost in a single night's storm. They would be blown over and never heard from again.

THE FISHERMEN'S MEMORIAL
BY LEONARD CRASKE
This harborside tribute to all the Gloucester fishermen who have lost their lives at sea over the centuries was made in 1925. A plaque beneath the statue reads: "They That Go Down To The Sea In Ships 1623–1923."

While fishing is still extremely dangerous, switching from sail to engines was one of the many technological changes that have made fishing a little less risky. Other changes include improved weather forecasting, cell phones, and special suits that keep fishermen warm and afloat in the water if their boat sinks or capsizes.

ON THE WEST COAST OF THE UNITED STATES, regulators have had some success in banning dragging in large patches of the ocean. There again, the distrust of foreigners helped, since most of the largest draggers were foreign owned. But the idea of closing off certain parts of the ocean to bottom draggers does seem to have a future.

THE BIGGEST HOPE FOR BANNING BOTTOM DRAGGING IS THE MARKETPLACE WHERE FISH IS SOLD.

If offered the choice between buying a fish caught in a net and one caught on a hook and line, most people would prefer the line-caught fish if they could see them. Net-caught fish can spend hours together, thousands of them—slithering, squirming, slapping one another—crushed against the net so that they arrive at the market scratched and bruised.

Until recently, the fish-selling business operated with very little inspection. Now, however, there's a growing trend toward selling fish in what are called "display auctions." At these auctions, all of the fish are sorted by species and fishery. So cod from a bottom dragger would be in a different bin than cod caught on a hook and line.

What people are finding in display auctions around the world is that fish that are caught on a hook and line are fetching higher prices than net-caught fish. What that means is that there is a real financial incentive for fishermen to abandon bottom dragging for the old-fashioned method of hook-and-line fishing. Because fishermen are being asked to catch fewer fish, their only hope for survival is to be paid more for the fewer fish they catch.

But there is another incentive. What today's fishermen want more than anything is to be set free from regulations. It's not that they want to destroy the sea—they simply want to be free. The great joy of the world's most dangerous job, why fishermen have always been willing to endure this hard life, is because no one has ever told them what to do.

That is not true anymore. It is not just the quotas or the restrictions on days at sea and where they can fish or the restrictions on the type of fishing gear they're allowed to use: It's a combination of all these rules and regulations. Today's fisherman is overwhelmed with regulations.

But fishermen who employ the old methods, such as hook-and-line fishing—or even harpooning—don't need to have nearly as many regulations. It would be impossible for hook-and-line fishermen to CATCH AS MANY FISH as they would have caught using bottom draggers, so they WOULDN'T HAVE TO WORRY about quotas or regulators.

AND WHAT'S EVEN BETTER IS THAT THE FISH THAT WERE CAUGHT MIGHT COMMAND TWO OR THREE TIMES THE PRICE PER POUND THAN FISH CAUGHT BY A BOTTOM DRAGGER, SO THE SAME AMOUNT OF MONEY WOULD BE MADE FOR FEWER FISH. IS THIS NOT THE FUTURE?

KRAM

AILAT

THE WHALES EVENTUALLY ALL DIED OFF, AND THE OCEAN LOST ITS SONG.

AILAT GREW UP, AND STUDIED TO BECOME AN OCEAN SCIENTIST, LIKE HER FATHER, KRAM.

SOMEWHERE IN THE WORLD, THERE HAS TO STILL BE A *LIVING* CORAL REEF. I'LL GO THERE, STUDY, AND PROTECT IT!

IF I ONLY KNEW WHERE TO LOOK.

I'VE STUDIED REEFS IN THE PACIFIC. THERE MUST BE ONE OR TWO LEFT THERE.

THE CENTRAL PACIFIC BASIN!

GOOD THINKING, AILAT!

I'M SURE THERE'S ONE STILL ALIVE AROUND HERE.

HAWAIIAN ISLANDS

MARSHALL ISLANDS

KINGMAN REEF!

PAPUA NEW GUINEA

KINGMAN REEF

KIRIBATI

SAMOA

IT WAS DISCOVERED BY A CONNECTICUT SEA CAPTAIN, AND IS A U.S. TERRITORY.

WASN'T KINGMAN REEF USED AS A SITE FOR TESTING NUCLEAR WEAPONS?

YES, A LONG TIME AGO -- BUT IN 2001, IT BECAME A WILDLIFE REFUGE.

IT'S PROBABLY THE MOST REMOTE SPOT ON EARTH!

THAT'S WHAT SAVED IT.

THERE WAS NO LAND OR FRESH WATER ANYWHERE AROUND KINGMAN REEF. HAWAII, THE CLOSEST ISLAND, WAS MORE THAN 1,000 MILES NORTH.

AILAT HAD TO LIVE ON THE BOAT AND COULDN'T STAY LONG, DUE TO KINGMAN REEF'S REMOTENESS.

BIRDS!

BUT IT WAS SURROUNDED BY BEAUTIFUL BLUE WATER, A COLORFUL, LIVING REEF, AND LOTS OF REAL FISH!

I CAN'T LET ANYONE DESTROY THIS ONE LAST PLACE!

TO BE CONTINUED ....

CHAPTER NINE

HOW POLLUTION IS KILLING FISH, TOO

The face of Nature may be compared to a yielding surface, with ten thousand sharp wedges packed close together and driven inwards by incessant blows, sometimes one wedge being struck, and then another with greater force.
—Charles Darwin, ON THE ORIGIN OF SPECIES

So they've tried to limit the effects of overfishing over the years with regulations, and to some extent some of these measures have proven successful— But why are the fish populations still shrinking? Clearly something is going wrong. The destruction continues.

WHILE THERE IS STILL MUCH OVERFISHING in the world, many of the traditional fishing grounds within 200-mile limits are tightly regulated. Most of the fishing fleets of Europe and North America have been following all the regulations that were handed to them. And despite a few successes here and there, the fish populations are not rebuilding satisfactorily. Fishermen have made tremendous sacrifices without seeing their stocks become healthy once more.

Part of the problem is that we too easily forget that all of human activity, not only fishing, affects marine life. For centuries, pollution—human waste, garbage, the poisonous by-products of industry—were dumped into the sea. Large ports, such as Boston, New York, and San Francisco, as well as the big ports of Europe, Asia, Africa—most of the world—are polluted. And this pollution has washed into the sea. So have the hazardous chemicals used in industrial agriculture to kill weeds and insects. When it rains, these poisons wash into the rivers and continue on to the sea. Some of the most polluted parts of the ocean are near the mouths of great rivers.

There are areas of the sea called dead zones, where large amounts of phytoplankton die from pollution and, as they rot, they use up all the oxygen in the water. Fish cannot live in water without oxygen.

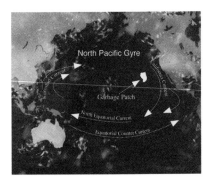

GREAT PACIFIC GARBAGE PATCH
In a number of places where ocean currents meet, there are concentrations of garbage, mostly plastics that cannot be readily absorbed by natural processes the way organic debris can. Instead, the plastics have broken down into suspended particles that cannot break down any further. These patches are sometimes referred to as plastic islands, though they are not solid masses that can be walked on. Sometimes there are recognizable objects such as a chair or a satellite dish, but mostly they are made up of small particles of plastic strewn together. The largest known patch, the Great Pacific Garbage Patch, is in the north central Pacific Ocean, the area between Japan and the United States, with garbage from both countries contributing. Estimates of the size of this patch vary from twice the size of the United States to only an eighth of that size. The patch is fed by debris from both land and ships, and the ocean currents carry it to a point where it becomes a fairly stable mass.

Many of the industrial pollutants in the ocean do not break down in water, so they move through the water unchanged, looking for the fatty tissues of plants and animals in which to deposit their components.

Over the past century, tremendous quantities of petroleum have spilled into the oceans. Some has been the result of thoughtless dumping by industry, but a great deal of it has been by accident. Much of this has been caused by accidents to oil tankers, huge ships used to transport hundreds of thousands of gallons of petroleum. It would be safer for the oceans if oil was transported in smaller ships, but oil companies argue that this would make oil far more expensive.

The public first became aware of this problem in 1967 when one of the so-called supertankers, *Torrey Canyon*, accidentally dumped 100 thousand tons of oil off the British coast, causing tremendous damage for many years along the coasts of Britain and France. In 1989, a tanker called the *Exxon Valdez* broke up in Prince William Sound, Alaska, which had been a pristine subarctic paradise for a wide range of fish, shellfish, mammals, and birds. The accident seriously damaged the entire life system of the Arctic. Although the United States passed legislation requiring all newly built tankers to have a double hull after the *Exxon Valdez* disaster, in the hopes of avoiding a repeat of that kind of catastrophe, the damage had already been done. When the oil reaches the shoreline some parts of the oil evaporate, leaving behind the heaviest components and turning the oil into tar.

OIL SINKS INTO MARSHES AND BEACHES, AND REMAINS THERE FOR YEARS.

But even in areas that are relatively easy to clean up, the damage from oil spills has been recorded for decades after the spill. Fish and shellfish developed abnormal characteristics including, in some cases, an inability to reproduce.

In 1969, the barge *Florida* broke up off of Cape Cod, Massachusetts, and dumped 200 thousand gallons of diesel fuel into a famous resort area. The disaster received a lot of press attention because the same year an offshore oil-rig accident covered another famous beach, in Santa Barbara, California, with black, heavy crude, which is really thick oil. In Cape Cod, thousands of fish, shellfish, and birds died. But after some months of work, the area was cleaned up, as was Santa Barbara. The wildlife came back, the tourists returned, Cape Cod recovered, and the incident was largely forgotten. But forty years later, scientists at the nearby Woods Hole Oceanographic Institution went into a Cape Cod salt marsh and found that the mud just below the surface still smelled of oil. Fiddler crabs were no longer digging deep holes, instead stopping when they hit the oil layer and then digging sideways. They appeared to be drunk from the oil fumes.

DRILLING OIL UNDER THE SEA ALSO POSES TREMENDOUS RISKS.

Such accidents do not happen often, but when they do, with disastrous results, it becomes clear that oil companies either cannot or do not have adequate safety practices to prevent such accidents. The world was once again reminded of this in 2010, a time when the idea of increasing such oil drilling in the sea was gaining popularity. Suddenly on April 20, an oil rig operating in the Gulf of Mexico exploded, killing eleven platform workers and unleashing the largest oil spill in history. Until the leak was plugged up on July 15, the well was leaking about two million gallons of oil every day. The exact amount, possibly more or less, is not known, but it was the equivalent of a major oil tanker disaster every day for three months.

The leak left an oil slick in the Gulf of Mexico that was estimated to be 2,500 square miles, though storms will widen it. There is also much more oil left under the surface and not visible. Unlike the Santa Barbara accident, this is not thick heavy oil but a lighter product known as "sweet crude," which is not only more toxic but very difficult to gather and remove and it is certain that

SOME OF THIS OIL WILL REMAIN IN THE SEA FOR THOUSANDS OF YEARS.

GULF SHORES, ALABAMA (JUNE 12, 2010)
Beaches all along the Gulf Coast were covered
with oil in the months following the
Deepwater Horizon explosion.

The Gulf of Mexico is an important breeding ground for fish, birds, and marine mammals and the long-range effect of this accident on the life of these animals, the ecology of the ocean, and if Darwin is understood, the entire natural order of the planet, is beyond the ability of science to measure.

The Gulf of Mexico disaster was a failure of both private industry and government. The responsible oil company, British Petroleum, had failed to follow the safest possible procedures in an attempt to reduce operating expenses. But the government agencies that were expected to regulate offshore drilling and make sure it was safe did not object to British Petroleum's approach. British Petroleum had a record of negligence. In October 2007, BP was fined twenty million dollars for the Prudhoe Bay oil spill. The oil company had ignored warnings by workers of a corroded pipeline in its drilling operation on the North Slope of Alaska, an area with a fragile environment rich in wildlife. On March 2, 2006, a quarter-inch hole was discovered in a pipeline in Prudhoe Bay. More than 200 thousand gallons of oil leaked out. BP has paid a twelve-million-dollar federal criminal fine, four million dollars in criminal restitution to the state, and four million dollars for Arctic research. BP's local subsidiary, BP Exploration (Alaska) Inc., was placed on probation for three years. British Petroleum also drills in the North Sea, historic but badly overharvested fishing grounds. Fishermen, recognizing the potential disaster, vehemently opposed offshore oil drilling and successfully blocked a plan to drill off of New England.

UNLESS THE WORLD REDUCES ITS USE OF OIL AND TURNS TO RENEWABLE ENERGY SOURCES, SUCH AS SOLAR AND WIND POWER, THERE ARE CERTAIN TO BE MORE DISASTERS LIKE THIS IN THE OCEANS.

Experts who analyze the oil industry say that most of the oil in the world that can be taken easily is running out and oil companies will increasingly extract oil from riskier and more difficult places. This means, unless it is banned, not only more offshore drilling, but drilling in fragile environments like the Arctic, and places where accidents can easily occur. One of the biggest oil discoveries of recent years is a vast pool under a mile of ocean off of Brazil. Known as pre-salt oil, this enormous pool of oil must be drilled not only in deep ocean waters, but under a mile of unstable shifting seabed made of salt, sand, and rock. This oil field is many times more likely to lead to an accident than was the Gulf of Mexico oil field.

IT'S NOT JUST BIG OIL SPILLS THAT have catastrophic results on the ocean ecosystems. Some of the deadliest pollutants, such as mercury and polychlorinated biphenyls, known as PCBs, are extremely difficult to ever clean up. PCBs are used in the manufacture of electrical equipment, paints, motor oil, plastics, floor finish, and numerous other household items. In the United States, until such practices were banned in 1979, these pollutants entered the land and consequently the sea, from waste produced during manufacturing. Since the PCBs do not break down, most of it is still in the environment.

More has been added from illegal dumping, leakage from landfills, and consumer products with PCB content being thrown away by the individuals using them. PCBs travel long distances in soil, air, and water and have been found all over the world in places far from where they entered the environment.

THE SMALLEST ANIMALS EAT THESE POISONS. AND THEN THE LARGER ANIMALS THAT EAT THE SMALLER ANIMALS GET THESE POISONS— BUT THEY DON'T JUST EAT ONE ANIMAL AT A TIME, THEY EAT MASSIVE QUANTITIES OF THESE ANIMALS.

These larger animals now have more poisons in their systems than the little ones did, so that by the time you get high up in the food chain, the concentration of poison has become much stronger in an individual animal. The largest fish will have eaten large quantities of the contaminated smaller fish, which makes the large fish dangerous to eat for the animal at the top of the food chain—which is us.

SEVERAL POISONOUS METALS, INCLUDING MERCURY, CHROMIUM, AND LEAD, HAVE MADE THEIR WAY INTO THE OCEANS—AND THEIR FOOD CHAIN—IN MUCH THE SAME WAYS AS PCBs HAVE.

These metals are what is known in chemistry as elements. As of 2009, there were 118 elements. Most of the poisonous metal elements, such as copper, mercury, and lead, have been known and used for thousands of years, though it was not until more recent times that it was understood that people were being poisoned by the use of these elements in pipes, dishes, and cooking pots. Once introduced to an environment, it is very difficult to get rid of elements because they cannot be broken down any further. Water, for instance, can be broken down into the two elements hydrogen and oxygen that together make up H_2O, and table salt is made of sodium and chloride. But hydrogen, oxygen, sodium, and chloride are all elements and cannot be broken down into anything else.

In some cases, children with low school performance have been tested and found to have high levels of mercury from eating contaminated fish. Women who are pregnant are warned to avoid eating large quantities of bigger fish, such as tuna, because of the possibility of ingesting too much mercury, which is potentially quite harmful to a baby in its mother's womb. This is especially sad because otherwise, the natural content of such fish is considered quite healthy, full of proteins that used to be quite beneficial to humans. But these poisons also seem to have a profound effect on fish populations and, although there has not been enough research on this, one of the side effects appears to be a reduced ability to reproduce.

While oil by-products, PCBs, and mercury have received the most attention, there are large quantities of other similar pollutants. Without anyone taking much notice, chromium has become another major pollutant of the seas.

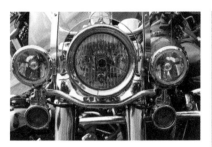

DETAIL OF A MOTORCYCLE
Chromium is what gives that high polish to motorcycle and car parts, kitchen fixtures, tools—and just about everything else. It is a naturally lustrous, hard metal that is very resistant to corrosion.

Chromium, like mercury, is a metal, an element—known in chemistry by the symbol Cr. Unlike most of the poisonous metal elements, this one has not been known for thousands of years but was only discovered in 1797. It takes a very shiny polish, is extremely hard, and resists corrosion. Bronze weapons found in burial pits in China, which archaeologists have dated from the late third century B.C., showed no sign of corrosion because the bronze tips of crossbow bolts and swords found at the site were coated with chromium. It is this quality that makes it extremely valuable to a wide range of industries. It is added to steel to make it rust resistant. It gives color and opaqueness to paints. Because of its ability to take a shine, it is used as a protective coating on car parts, plumbing fixtures, and furniture parts. It's used in many kinds of kitchenwares, including knives, and is an important element in textile dyes, jet engines, treating wood to protect it from termites, high-performance audiotape, gasoline, and curing leather. The paint used to make school buses yellow is made with chromium. And it tints glass green. In short, it is in almost everything we manufacture on this planet—and unfortunately, it has ended up in the sea, the last receptacle of industrial pollution. Even those who study sea pollution have been surprised at how much chromium pollution is present nowadays.

Although small amounts of chromium are needed by human bodies to process sugar, and there is even a disease called chromium deficiency, excessive amounts of chromium are poisonous to both humans and fish. It is known to cause cancer and damage to kidneys, liver, and blood cells, but there was little public awareness of the issue until 2000 when the film *Erin Brockovich* was released. Based on a true incident in California, it is the story of an entire community that was poisoned by industrial chromium seeping into the ground water.

Research has shown chromium-based products to cause chromosome damage to hamsters. Marine biologists have also found that it has the potential to alter the DNA of fish. Deoxyribonucleic acid (DNA) contains the genetic instructions used in the development and functioning of all known living organisms.

ALTERATIONS IN DNA ARE KEY TO EVOLUTION. IF THEY CAUSE SUCCESSFUL CHANGES TO A SPECIES IN THE ENVIRONMENT, THE SPECIES WILL CONTINUE. IT MIGHT TAKE MILLIONS OF YEARS TO SEE THE SUBTLE CHANGES CAUSED BY ALTERATIONS IN DNA IF A SPECIES IS SUCCESSFUL. BUT IT WOULDN'T TAKE THAT LONG IF THE ALTERATIONS TO THE DNA WERE NOT SUCCESSFUL.

THERE IS STRONG EVIDENCE THAT DNA DAMAGE IN FISH IS REDUCING THEIR ABILITY TO REPRODUCE AT ALL, WHICH COULD CAUSE FISH SPECIES TO DISAPPEAR EVEN WITHOUT OUR OVERFISHING OF THEM.

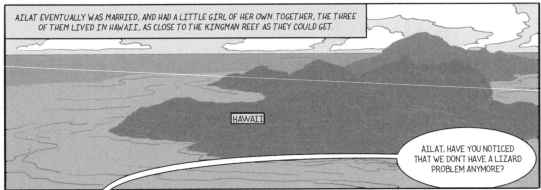

AILAT EVENTUALLY WAS MARRIED, AND HAD A LITTLE GIRL OF HER OWN. TOGETHER, THE THREE OF THEM LIVED IN HAWAII, AS CLOSE TO THE KINGMAN REEF AS THEY COULD GET.

HAWAII

AILAT, HAVE YOU NOTICED THAT WE DON'T HAVE A LIZARD PROBLEM ANYMORE?

THEY USED TO BE ALL OVER THE HOUSE!

COME TO THINK OF IT, I HAVEN'T REALLY SEEN THEM MUCH OUTSIDE, EITHER.

LOOK! THERE USED TO BE BEETLES & ALL KINDS OF BUGS CRAWLING AROUND ON THESE TREES!

WHERE ARE THEY?

WHERE ARE THE BIRDS?

WHAT'S GOING ON, AILAT?

IT'S SPREAD TO THE LAND NOW.

TO BE CONTINUED...

CHAPTER TEN

HOW GLOBAL WARMING IS ALSO KILLING FISH

Climate plays an important part in determining the average number of a species.
—Charles Darwin, ON THE ORIGIN OF SPECIES

During the last century, the average temperature of the Earth's surface and the air near the surface rose between 0.6 and 0.9 degrees centigrade. The temperature appears to be continuing to rise and most scientists agree that a rise of two degrees would bring about catastrophic changes. Polar ice caps would melt and sea levels would rise enough to overflow many coastlines, ports, and major cities.

THE PRIMARY CAUSE OF THIS RISE in temperature is thought to be an increase in greenhouse gases, a group of gases that warm the Earth to a temperature that makes life possible. The main greenhouse gases in the earth's atmosphere are water vapor, carbon dioxide, methane, nitrous oxide, and ozone. It is a natural process in which the gases hold in the heat in much the same way as glass does in a greenhouse. Without greenhouse gases, the planet would be too cold for most life. The problem is that since the 1800s, human beings have been steadily increasing the amount of greenhouse gases emitted into the atmosphere through industrial activities like the burning of fossils fuels—especially coal and oil products. And that has been compounded by the cutting down of forests that we have been doing on a grand scale for centuries. When a forest is cleared, the burning that is commonly practiced or even the debris that rots, emit carbon dioxide. Enough forests are cleared every year for this to have become an important source of carbon dioxide.

Global warming has already had observable impact on wild animals. One of the best-known problems is the polar bear losing its habitat as Arctic ice melts. Human beings, always true to their own biological class, have studied the problems of mammals—but little attention has been paid to

the impact of global warming on fish. One American study showed that global warming was causing entire fish populations to move north in search of colder waters. Subarctic fish are heading toward the Arctic. Temperate-water fish are moving into the subarctic. Subtropical fish are moving toward more temperate zones. And tropical fish are moving toward the subtropics. This is particularly bad news for the tropics, which has special systems, such as coral reefs, that are very valuable to the natural order of the oceans.

People imagine warm seas to be rich in fish because the land seems to be so rich in vegetation. But the cold seas are much richer in fish than the warmer ones because

FISH PREFER COLDER WATERS. THE WARMING OF THE SEAS IS A CRISIS FOR FISH.

IF THE SEAS ARE WARMING AND ICE IS MELTING, THIS MEANS THAT THE MELTED ICE, WHICH IS FRESHWATER, WILL MAKE THE SEAS LESS SALTY.

It is known that most fish live not only in a specific temperature range but in a specific degree of saltiness, known as the salinity of water. The proper salinity of water is essential to the survival of fish.

It is also known that many fish take a certain change in temperature as a signal to begin reproducing. Changes in water temperature and salinity may be confusing some fish so that they have stopped reproducing. There is also some evidence that excessive carbon is being introduced into the oceans and particularly the deepwater ocean where fish have been less exposed to change and are not as adaptable. Some research indicates that excessive carbon may slow down the growth rate in fish, and because growth correlates with egg production and the ability of fish populations to reproduce, this, too, bodes very badly for these deepwater fish populations.

AND AS DARWIN WOULD POINT OUT, A CHANGE IN THIS POPULATION WOULD IMPACT OTHER FISH POPULATIONS AND SPIRAL ACROSS THE PLANET.

YEARS LATER, AILAT TOOK HER HUSBAND AND DAUGHTER TO MEET HER LONGTIME FRIENDS, FRANK & SALVY.

HOW DO YOU KNOW FRANK & SALVY, MOMMY?

GRANDPA USED TO TAKE ME FISHING WITH THEM WHEN I WAS A LITTLE GIRL, JUST LIKE YOU!

THEY MUST BE TALENTED FISHERMEN TO BE ABLE TO MAKE A LIVING AT IT.

THEY'RE... RESOURCEFUL.

FRANK AND SALVY WERE NO LONGER FISHING TOGETHER, BUT EACH OF THEM HAD HIS OWN BOAT.

WHO WOULD HAVE GUESSED? FOLKS ARE EATING JELLYFISH MORE EVERY DAY!

WHAT ABOUT SALVY?

I HUNT SEA TURTLES NOW! SOME WEIGH UP TO 1,000 POUNDS!

ISN'T IT GREAT? LEATHERBACK TURTLES. THEY WERE GONE FROM THIS AREA LONG BEFORE OUR TIME, BUT NOW, THEY'RE BACK!

JUST PROVES THAT YOU CAN'T KILL OFF NATURE.

WHAT MADE THEM COME BACK?

JELLYFISH! SEA TURTLES EAT THEM RIGHT UP!

HEY, LET'S ALL GO TO LEO'S FOR DINNER TONIGHT! THEY MAKE GREAT TURTLE STEAK, TURTLE SOUP, JELLYFISH SALAD...

GRANDPA USED TO TAKE ME TO LEO'S WHEN I WAS A LITTLE GIRL, AND BIG, WHITE BIRDS WOULD TRY TO STEAL THE FISH RIGHT OFF OUR PLATES!

MOMMY,

WHAT'S A FISH?

THE END

CHAPTER ELEVEN

TIME TO WAKE UP AND SMELL THE FISH

Judging from the past, we may safely infer that not one living species will transmit its unaltered likeness to a distant futurity. And of the species now living very few will transmit progeny of any kind to a far distant futurity; for the manner in which all organic beings are grouped, shows that the greater number of species of each genus, and all the species of many genera, have left no descendants, but have become utterly extinct.

—Charles Darwin, ON THE ORIGIN OF SPECIES

If Darwin is right, we are all doomed. All species will have modifications that will develop into new species, and the original species will become extinct.

WHERE THERE WERE ONCE DINOSAURS, there are now birds. Some may even argue that the birds are an improvement. But Darwin was talking about a process that, he repeatedly pointed out, was extremely slow—changes that took place over millions of years. What we are seeing today are changes caused by humans that will take only years. And as we cause the extinction of other species, we are hastening our own extinction.

There is broad recognition that we need to act. But can we agree on what to do? Fishermen are among the most vocal groups speaking out against pollution and global warming. They make the perfectly valid point that we will never understand the problems of fish if we look only at fishing. But environmentalists, fearing the fishermen will start claiming that the decline of the oceans' fish is the result of pollution and global warming alone, continue to point at overfishing as the major culprit.

The truth is, both groups are right. Even while great strides have been made toward regulating the fishing industry and preventing overfishing, there are still fishing companies that search the globe for international waters or fishing grounds controlled by desperately poor countries. They then pay the poor country to be allowed to fish their waters without regulations

In 1950, more than 90 percent of the fish caught by commercial fishermen were taken from the Northern Hemisphere.

Today, places in the Southern Hemisphere, such as Peru and various African nations, have some of the most productive fishing grounds in the world. That's because other countries are sending their ships away from their own tired, depleted waters to fish in their waters. They are underpaying many of these impoverished countries for the rights to their finite resources.

or restrictions. Some of the most destructive fishing is done by wealthy countries off the coasts of poor ones.

IT IS TOO EASILY FORGOTTEN THAT nature will operate by its own rules.

We can see our mistakes and correct them, but nature does not always wait for our corrections. Nature does not like empty spaces. When a species becomes scarce in one area, another species that eats the same food will come in and take its place. Then there is not enough food for the original species to ever come back.

IN THE OCEANS OF THE WORLD, WE ARE KILLING THE SPECIES WE MOST APPRECIATE, and those species are being replaced by ones that we do not care for. In the dead zones, now that the fish and the oxygen are gone, the only life is certain types of bacteria that don't need oxygen.

BEING MAMMALS, WE TEND TO DO A BETTER JOB OF PROTECTING FELLOW MAMMALS THAN PROTECTING FISH.

So we have stopped the killing of seals and there are now many seals. But seals eat cod, which we have allowed to become scarce. The seals make them even scarcer and soon there will not be enough food for seals. But nature has its own way of regulating. Hundreds of gray seals have moved into the harbor of Chatham on Cape Cod with the result that inshore cod have been disappearing. Scientists believe that hundreds of years ago, before they were hunted, seals lived in Chatham Harbor. But that was also before cod was hunted with large-scale commercial fishing, so there was enough food to support the seal herd. But now, to the horror of the tourists who loved the seals, the little-known Atlantic great white shark has moved to Chatham and is eating the seals.

SPINNER DOLPHIN
(*Stenella longirostris*)

It is estimated that up to two million dolphins have been killed as a result of by-catch by tuna fishermen until Congress passed the Marine Mammal Protection Act in 1972. Even so, the Eastern Spinner Dolphin is now considered a "depleted" species: Its population stock is below its optimum sustainable population.

In the eastern tropical Pacific from San Diego to Peru and Hawaii, yellowfin tuna swim with dolphins, a smaller species of whale. We are not sure why. Tuna fishermen used to kill enormous numbers of dolphins as by-catch, but after a huge public outcry, mammal-loving people have banned the killing of dolphins. But the dolphin population has not been increasing and most scientists think that is because the killing of tuna continues and the dolphin need the tuna to survive. Some scientists think the dolphins help the tuna to find the smaller fish that they both eat. Or it could be that the tuna warn them and help them to avoid predators. Or they may both be following birds. Do the tuna and the dolphins drive baitfish up to the surface by their activity but only find them because dolphins can hear the birds crashing down and feeding? This may be an example of fish, birds, and mammals relying on one another. Now that we have upset nature's balance it becomes

EXTREMELY COMPLICATED TO PUT IT RIGHT AGAIN.

WHAT CAN WE DO ABOUT THIS?

YOU COULD REFUSE TO EAT FISH

but this would not only deprive you of a very healthy food, it would not help. If you refuse to eat any fish, then there is no reward for those who fish in sustainable ways. Instead, you should eat fish, but only good fish, fish that were caught in sustainable fishing. The good news is that these varieties are usually the best-quality fish, the fish handled with the most care. The problem is, how do you know which fish come from good fisheries?

BEWARE OF FISH

that is very inexpensive. Cheap fish has usually been caught in careless ways.

BEWARE OF NEW TYPES OF FISH

that are suddenly being seen everywhere. That was the case of orange roughy. It was also the case with redfish. In 1981, Louisiana chef Paul Prudhomme invented a recipe for "blackened" redfish that called for rubbing spices on a redfish fillet and cooking it in a very hot cast-iron skillet so that the sides of the fish turned black. Redfish was a Gulf of Mexico sea drum, a fish that was not particularly popular. But suddenly, it seemed everyone wanted blackened redfish and in less than ten years, the annual catch of redfish in the Gulf went from 1.6 million pounds to more than seven million pounds. Federal regulators stepped in to limit the catch, and with the help of Prudhomme's campaign to save the redfish, a total collapse of the drum population in the Gulf was averted.

Another such case is Chilean sea bass, an unknown fish that suddenly appeared in restaurants and fish stores around the world. One reason this fish was little known is that it lives in the Southern Hemisphere, where there was very little large-scale commercial fishing until recent decades. Its real name is Patagonian toothfish and it is not a bass at all. For that matter, much of it isn't from Chile. The name was created to market the fish internationally. But like orange roughy, it is a slow-growing fish that does not reproduce until late in life. Because of that, it is extremely easy to overfish this population and very difficult to fish it sustainably. There are a few exceptions but it is generally overfished, and efforts to protect it have led to a great deal of illegal fishing in Antarctic seas that are difficult to patrol. The primary fishing technique used, long lines with many hooks running deep below the surface, entrap not only the fish but also the albatross,

PATAGONIAN TOOTHFISH
AKA CHILEAN SEA BASS
(*Dissostichus eleginoides*)

People didn't want to eat a fish
called the Patagonian toothfish
because it didn't sound very
appetizing. It wasn't until some
clever marketing person changed
the named to Chilean sea bass
that this fish became wildly
popular and is now in danger of
being overfished into extinction.

which is an endangered bird, and drowns other seabirds as well.

SO IF WE ARE TO EAT FISH RESPONSIBLY, how do we know which are the good fish, the ones caught in a sustainable way that is not destructive, and which are the bad ones? This is an extremely difficult task, but one that we have a moral obligation to try to undertake. Numerous organizations publish lists of fish that should not be eaten and fish that can be eaten. The problem with these lists is that the people who compile them do not have the means to determine this. It is not a question of which fish you can eat—haddock is good and swordfish is bad. You have to distinguish between the haddock caught in a dragger net, and the haddock caught on a line, and between lines with two hooks and lines with fifty, and between netted swordfish and harpooned swordfish. You have to have a staff of hundreds that goes to sea with every fishery in the world. You would also have to update this list several times a year by returning to each fishery regularly to make sure the fishery has not changed its practices or the environmental circumstances have not changed. If this book were to include a list of good and bad fish, the list would be hopelessly out of date by the time the book was published. To call for the boycott of a sustainable fishery simply because they are catching the same species of fish as other unsustainable fisheries is not only a terrible injustice to the fishermen who went to the trouble and expense—and sometimes danger—to fish correctly but it also makes fishermen feel that there is no incentive to catch fewer fish in a sustainable way.

There are some organizations that do offer some guidance about which fish are good fish to eat—and which aren't. These organizations have been working with scientists and fishermen on developing better ways of monitoring the oceans' fish stocks and coming up with new ways of motivating fishermen to practice sustainable fishing.

MARINE STEWARDSHIP COUNCIL

www.msc.org

In 1997, the Marine Stewardship Council (MSC) was founded by the World Wildlife Fund, a leading environmental group, and Unilever, a leading international seafood retailer. The idea was to give the concept of sustainable fishing commercial value in the fish market. The proof of its success is that fisheries around the world have volunteered to be examined and

If you see this label on the seafood you or your parents are about to purchase, you know that it has been fished through sustainable means.

have their operations assessed against the MSC's strict environmental standards. Depending on the complexity of the assessment, fisheries pay between 15 thousand and 120 thousand dollars to the independent certifier to undergo assessment. If a fishery is deemed sustainable, it becomes certified and can use the blue MSC ecolabel on its seafood products. The MSC ecolabel tells the consumer that this is a fish that can be eaten without harming the environment.

The MSC program is important because it gives the conscientious consumer a way to verify the fish, and it gives conscientious fishermen a way to be commercially rewarded for their efforts. Since 2000, more than a hundred fisheries have been certified worldwide. While this represents a significant and growing amount of the total wild-caught fish production globally, there are still many fisheries in need of assessment. Also, the already certified operations must be constantly reappraised. All certified fisheries have annual audits, and are completely reassessed every five years to make sure their fishing practices are still sustainable.

Some certifications are controversial. One Chilean sea bass fishery was certified, for instance, which upset some environmentalists because it would have been much simpler and clearer to simply say "Don't eat Chilean sea bass." In 2010, one group harvesting krill in the Antarctic received MSC certification on the grounds that the fraction of the krill in that area that this group was harvesting did not injure the population. But some environmentalists argued that a larger krill harvest might have a negative impact, and the entire practice should be banned.

MONTEREY BAY AQUARIUM

www.montereybayaquarium.org

The Monterey Bay Aquarium in California has a "Seafood Watch" program that informs the public about which fish to eat and which to avoid in each region. It even attempts to distinguish between environmentally sound fish farming, like farmed striped bass, and harmful farming practices, such as farmed salmon. Their approach is easy for consumers to understand, but by labeling a species rather than an individual fishery, they do occasionally lump a few good fisheries in with the bad ones. Since 2000, they have been publishing a pocket guide that divides fish into three categories: a green list of fish that can be eaten without harming the environment, a yellow list of less preferable but still acceptable alternatives, and a red

This is the cover of the Seafood Watch pocket guide. You can find the entire guide on page 177.

list of those fish to be avoided. As of 2011, they had 35 million copies of this guide in circulation. This list, which serves as the basis for many of the other lists around the country, is monitored by fifteen people, including seven scientists, who read published reports and only on rare occasions go to sea to inspect. They are intended for consumers, but also for restaurants and even some fish wholesalers. It's updated twice a year, so check the website for the most recent lists.

CAPE COD COMMERCIAL HOOK FISHERMEN'S ASSOCIATION

www.ccchfa.org

In 1991, a group of Cape Cod fishermen centered around the town of Chatham formed an organization that they called Cape Cod Commercial Hook Fishermen's Association. They would fish for bottom fish, especially cod and haddock, but only with hooks and lines. They gave a brand name to their line-caught cod: Chatham cod. At auction, top prices go to Chatham cod not because it is environmentally friendly, though it is, but because it is carefully handled and landed fresh. So this is good for everyone: The fishermen make more money catching fewer fish, consumers get healthier fish AND support a fishery that is trying very hard to do a good thing.

But there are still a few problems. Not all the cod landed in Chatham is line-caught. Fishermen have addressed this problem by labeling the line-caught fish "line-caught Chatham cod." Generally speaking, when you buy line-caught Chatham cod, you are supporting the sustainable fishery movement.

THE NATURE CONSERVANCY

www.nature.org

Centered in Moro Bay, California, a project run by an environmental group, the Nature Conservancy, demonstrates what can be accomplished when environmentalists and commercial fishermen work together. In 2004, the Nature Conservancy started buying up permits for bottom draggers from fishermen who were finding their trade so unprofitable that they were looking for a way out. Eventually they controlled thirteen dragging permits. They went to the government fishery management and asked for an arrangement similar to the sector management experiment in New England, whereby they would be given an annual catch limit and manage it themselves. They turned the permits over to fishermen. Seven of them were changed into permits for line or trap fishing, another old-fashioned and traditionally sustainable technique. The other six continued to drag but with lightweight dragger nets that trawl for only twenty minutes rather than ten hours, and target very specific species while avoiding damage to the bottom. They divided their central California fishing grounds into an area for this light trawling, an area for line fishing, and 3.8 million acres of seabed in which no bottom dragging is allowed at all.

THERE ARE MANY INTERESTING AND ADMIRABLE sustainable fisheries. Albacore tuna is caught in San Diego by dropping bait in the water, sending the fish into a feeding frenzy, and hauling them up on unbaited hooks—an entirely sustainable approach. While most salmon is in decline, and most salmon farming is environmentally disastrous, in Alaska salmon fishing is well managed. Salmon is usually labeled in stores by its origin, which makes it easier for consumers to identify the good salmon from the bad—but many other sustainable fisheries are not so easy to identify. There is no label indicating the fish of Moro Bay, for instance, which are mainly various species of rockfish. Though most Chilean sea bass fisheries are not sustainable, which is why the Monterey Bay Aquarium's pocket guide recommends not eating ANY Chilean sea bass, there is one fishery in the south Georgia Islands that actually is sustainable and has been certified by the Marine Stewardship Council. That's why it's really important to log onto these websites to get a full picture of what's going on whenever possible. Of course, you can make it simple for yourself and just not eat troubled species like cod and Chilean sea bass, but then you are ignoring—rather than encouraging—the fishermen who are fishing it the right way. Before you protest, boycott, or urge others to take action, you have to investigate and make sure that the fish in question comes from a truly unsustainable fishery.

It cannot even be said that ALL farmed fish should be avoided, though earlier in this book I discussed why fish farms are not a good solution to the problem of overfishing. Certain fish, like Atlantic salmon, clearly should be avoided, but there are some well-managed freshwater fish farms, and shellfish farms can produce a good product that actually improves water quality.

A FEW SPECIES OF FISH ARE SO THREATENED, HOWEVER, THAT THEY SHOULD TRULY NEVER BE EATEN.

NEVER EAT ANY KIND OF SHARK.

They produce few offspring and mature very slowly, which makes them unable to survive commercial fishing.

NEVER EAT BLUEFIN TUNA.

This is a highly migratory fish and requires a great deal of international cooperation to regulate. It is not well managed, and is on the verge of being fished into extinction.

So what should you eat?

You should not only be eating fish from sustainable fisheries but you should be eating fish that is lower on the food chain. Most popular fish are fairly high on the marine food chain and, as a result, contain a great deal of pollutants, particularly heavy metals such as mercury. Sardines, anchovies, and herring are lower on the food chain, and much healthier. In California, sardines are so abundant with so little demand that they are being sold to fish farms for food. Luckily for us, sardines make an excellent food—rich in omega-3 fatty acids, which help boost immunity, reduce the risk of heart disease, stroke, and cancer. They are also especially important for pregnant and nursing women—and young children. Kids should definitely be eating more sardines.

WHAT ABOUT CANNED TUNA?

Canned tuna is the second most popular seafood in America, behind shrimp. The best is albacore tuna, which is from the most sustainable fishery and is sometimes labeled "solid white." The top-of-the line albacore is line-caught in the Pacific Ocean, in places like the San Diego fishery. The Marine Stewardship Council puts their MSC label on cans of albacore caught in this way. But although albacore is an environmentally safe choice, it is not a healthy one because it is a large fish, more than four feet long, high up on the food chain, and contains a high concentration of mercury and other pollutants.

MOST KIDS LIKE FISH STICKS. ARE THOSE O.K. TO EAT?

There are numerous conflicting stories about the origin of fish sticks. Claims in both England and Massachusetts of origins in the 1920s are clearly false because two things had to have been invented before the advent of fish sticks: a process for freezing food and a machine that automatically removed skin and bones from fish. The freezing food part came first. In 1929, a New York–born inventor named Clarence Birdseye, working out of Gloucester, Massachusetts, developed a commercial process for freezing food. In 1933, the filleting machine was developed for automatically removing skin and bones from fish.

The forerunner of fish sticks was fish fingers—strips of fish fillet that were breaded and frozen. With fish fingers, it mattered what the fish was because it could be recognized. So in the 1930s, when the British tried to market fish fingers from herring, they tested the market by also producing some fingers made from cod. To their surprise, they found that cod was far more popular.

Fish sticks also began with cod. Fish sticks are a block of frozen fillet run through a saw to make rectangular shapes. No particular fish is recognizable, but in Gloucester, where fish sticks began, cod was still cheap and plentiful—so it became the source of fish sticks when fish sticks first came on the scene in the early 1950s. Fish sticks were new and interesting enough that *Time* magazine actually did a story about the Birds Eye product in 1953.

Back then, there was another type of catch that was as abundant as cod—the redfish. A type of sea perch with no relationship to the red drum that is called redfish in the Gulf of Mexico (see page 150), the redfish was easier to fillet by machine than cod, and thus replaced cod as the main ingredient of fish sticks. But too many were caught in the thirty years following the invention of the filleting machine, and so by the 1960s, redfish had become scarce. That's when fish sticks started being made from cod again—or haddock, when cod got scarce.

Today cod, haddock, and most New England ground fish are too rare and expensive to be frozen, sliced, and sold inexpensively as unidentified fish sticks. New England companies such as Gorton's buy Pacific pollack, scooped up and frozen by large industrial bottom draggers and flown east to be sliced into sticks. But Pacific pollack may soon be going the way of Atlantic cod and redfish: overfished into scarcity.

What is it about fish sticks that leads to the destruction of fish stocks? It is two things: Fish sticks are a food product that disguises a natural ingredient. Such types of food lead to a lack of respect for the original source of the food. But also it is a very inexpensive way to eat fish. And attempts to harvest wild products inexpensively almost always lead to destruction because it is very difficult to find a cheap way of harvesting large quantities of wild fish in a sustainable way.

WE NEED MORE INFORMATION and we should demand it. When you or your family buy fish, ask the people who are selling it where it came from and how it was caught. Politely tell them that you really want to know these things before you choose a fish. The people who sell the fish may not have the answers to your questions—they usually don't—but the more we ask them, the more they will want to find the answers. More and more, fish markets are making it their business to supply information about their fish to their customers because it is good business. People pay more money for a fish they know something about and can appreciate. If we all buy fish that is only from sustainable fisheries, there will be more and more sustainable fisheries. When all fishing becomes sustainable fishing, as it was for centuries, the crisis will be over—or at least half-over. There will still be the huge problems of climate change and pollution to be solved before fish—and the way of life of our coastlines and the seas themselves—will have been saved. A fish market that supplies all the necessary information, an ice counter with fully identified and certified fish, is the first big step.

If your local fish market insists on selling fish that is clearly wrong to sell, do not approach this merchant as an adversary. First, make absolutely certain that they are indeed buying fish from harmful fisheries. Remember that the oceans are so complex and little known that there are few certainties. But if they still refuse to change their ways, try to talk to them about their products, tell them why you think this is such an important issue for you—and for them. And if they still don't listen, you could take things into your own hands.

YOU CAN ORGANIZE A PICKET LINE.

A group of kids in front of a store or restaurant with signs saying "Do not patronize this store. They are selling endangered species," could be extremely effective. When kids show that they care about an issue, it has a tremendous impact on adults who wonder why they aren't more involved. But you must be extremely careful to act in a polite and respectful way so that you are seen as dedicated kids with a strong conscience, and not rowdy kids trying to make trouble, which is the usual accusation used to dismiss the opinions of young people.

If you are in a restaurant, feel free to ask your waiter if the seafood being offered on the menu is from a sustainable fishery. The waiter probably won't know, so he or she may offer to ask the chef. Since it is the chef who usually buys the food to cook, you will be letting the chef know, just by asking your question, that there are people who really take this kind of thing seriously. If the chef is unable to tell you where the fish on the menu came from, then leave a polite note explaining that you decided not to eat the fish at this restaurant because you support sustainable fishing and will only eat fish that come from sustainable fisheries.

YOU CAN WRITE LETTERS TO ELECTED OFFICIALS.

Government plays a central role in the regulation of fish and yet only a few senators and congressional representatives from fishing districts show interest in this problem. Write your elected officals. In polite and not strident language tell your age, grade, where you go to school, and why you are worried about fish and the oceans and what you would like him or her to do about it. You can also write to express your concern about the use of oil for energy, oil spills, pollution, and global warming. Tell them that it is your future and they must do something. But if you want them to listen, make sure you tell them with courtesy and respect.

A great deal of the most abusive fishing takes place in the waters of other countries or in international waters. The only way to effect this is through diplomacy, so write your representatives and the president and tell them that you want this to be a priority in international relations. For example, the bluefin tuna, as we know, is in danger of extinction from fishing since it is a migratory fish and travels the globe, so it is impossible for one country to regulate. It can only be done by international cooperation. While the United States is doing all that it can to protect the bluefin tuna, other countries aren't always eager to comply. Japan, for instance, buys nearly 80 percent of the annual Atlantic bluefin catch to serve as gourmet sushi, and has been reluctant to comply with recommendations about bluefin tuna. But Japan is an important commercial nation with a very large economy that has extensive relations and frequent negotiations with the

United States. The only way to save the bluefin tuna is to get the other wealthy nations of the world to make a halt to bluefin tuna fishing a priority in their negotiations with Japan. Write your government officals and ask them to do this.

YOU CAN ALSO BECOME INVOLVED IN ENVIRONMENTAL GROUPS.

They are usually glad to get the help. But it is important to remember that when talking about the oceans, everything is complicated and there are few certain truths. Despite often sounding like enemies, fishermen and environmentalists are on the same side. Both groups want to save the oceans. Remember that fishermen were the first to talk about the issue, and they desperately want to solve the problem. They are certainly not always right, but any real solution will involve their cooperation so anyone who wants to help should be prepared to work constructively with them.

Like fishermen, environmental groups and scientists are not always right, either. When fishermen claim that environmentalists overstate things in order to raise more money, they are only slightly exaggerating. These groups are not only under intense pressure to raise money but they are also trying to get people's attention to get them involved. For both these reasons, it is tempting to oversimplify and overdramatize. Fishermen are quick to point out that these groups take money from organizations whose interests may not be entirely environmental. On the other hand, the fishermen who hurl these accusations would like us to forget that their primary interest is making a living from the sea, and their own commercial interests often lead them to slightly bend the truth in their favor.

Environmental groups are backed by scientists who work with them and try to inform them with the best information. Nevertheless, you can often get more accurate information directly from scientists than from the environmental groups. The problem is the information from scientists is often written in a way that makes it difficult to understand. You may need help from a teacher in understanding these scientific documents but they are often worth reading. Many biologists have their own websites or post their papers on other sites. You can use a search engine to find topics of interest.

In the back of this book, you will find a resource section with the names of some groups that work on marine issues.

ALL SUCCESSFUL SOCIAL MOVEMENTS are the product of long-term, patient planning. They succeed because a few courageous and determined people organize a movement with enough structure to take action. This was true of the movements to abolish slavery in several countries, the movements to gain basic rights for workers, the civil rights movement, the anti–Vietnam War movement, the environmental movement of the 1970s that laid the groundwork for environmental protection, the gay rights movement, the women's rights movement, and many other examples. An organization was always started first—then nurtured and grown—before becoming effective through action. Studying some of these movements—the civil rights movement from the early 1940s to the early 1960s is one of the most instructive examples—will give you ideas on how to develop your own movement to save the oceans. Of course, all movements are designed for the time and culture in which they operate. Your movement, unlike the civil rights movement, will utilize the Internet, e-mail, social networking sites such as Facebook and Twitter, and other modern tools that might not have been invented yet. But remember, in an age of electronic mass communication, face-to-face contact is, more than ever, the most effective way to reach someone. But the fundamentals of an organization remain the same.

SAVING THE PLANET TAKES A LOT OF WORK. But what could be more worthwhile? Most scientists agree that it is still not too late. But they also generally agree that there is a point when the damage will become irreversible and that we do not have many years, perhaps only a generation, to reach that point. That is why yours is a special generation, one faced with more responsibilities and more opportunities than any generation in history. You cannot afford to be passive. You have to learn about what is happening to the planet and you will have to act.

THE SURVIVAL OF NOT ONLY THE OCEANS BUT OF OUR WORLD IS AT STAKE.

RESOURCES

ENVIRONMENTAL GROUPS
WORKING ON MARINE ISSUES

Blue Ocean Institute
www.blueocean.org
Founded in 2003 by writer/activist Carl Safina, the seafood guide on their website shares many of the strengths and weaknesses of the Monterey Bay Aquarium's site. They, too, do not examine individual fisheries firsthand, but rely on published reports. They give considerable details on the various fisheries of many commercial species, but sometimes fail to mention the exceptions, the good sustainable fisheries of an otherwise menaced species. Generally, however, there is a lot of useful information here.

The Cousteau Society
www.cousteau.org and **www.cousteaukids.org**
Founded in 1973 by Jacques-Yves Cousteau (1910–1997), a pioneer scuba diver and underwater filmmaker, as well as one of the inventors of the aqua lung, The Cousteau Society is one of the major marine ecology organizations in the world. Cousteau himself dedicated his life to the exploration and preservation of the oceans and was one of the first and most prominent marine ecologists. He was equally concerned with environmental fights and with educating the general public, making 120 television documentaries and writing more than forty books.

Environmental Defense Fund
www.edf.org
Founded in 1967, this organization got started during the legal battle to ban the pesticide DDT. The Environmental Defense Fund teams lawyers with scientists to fight for the environment through the legal system. They have fought to save whales, implement global warming initiatives, and force McDonald's to use less packaging. Their website includes a "seafood selector," which lists environmentally friendly fish choices similar to that of the Monterey Bay Aquarium, as well as additional information on fisheries and marine pollution.

Greenpeace
www.greenpeace.org

Greenpeace is a Dutch-based organization founded in 1971. Although their missions statement says it "uses peaceful direct action and creative communication" to address global issues, their specialty seems to be confrontation, often putting their activists physically in harm's way. Many times, they know their activists will fail to stop the operations they are trying to intercept, but they continue because they also know that their aggressive and risky theatrics will garner important publicity. Through this approach, Greenpeace often does a commendable job of bringing issues to public attention, but their confrontational methods often make peaceful solutions seem impossible—and fail to promote meaningful dialogue between opposing parties. Ultimately, I find this counterproductive to the goals we talk about in this book—goals that can only be met if everyone works together.

Marine Stewardship Council
www.msc.org

Founded in 1995, the Marine Stewardship Council is the only organization that actually travels the seas and inspects fisheries. Their website provides a wealth of information, including a list of MSC certified "fish to eat" and a list of sustainable fisheries. When you click on a fish on this list, you are not told if it is good or bad, but which fisheries are fishing that species sustainably and where to buy their fish.

Monterey Bay Aquarium
www.montereybayaquarium.org

This is where you will find one of the leading lists of fish to eat and fish to avoid. Their Seafood Watch Guide (reproduced on the next pages) is meant to be quick and easy for kids and general consumers to understand, but can be a little misleading in its simplicity. The better thing to do is log on to their website to download updated lists. There is also a Seafood Watch app that's available for free. For more information and helpful links go to www.worldwithoutfishthebook.com or www.workman.com/worldwithoutfish.

     Also worthwhile is the MBA's Super Green List, a changing list of fish that are not only the best to eat from an environmental standpoint, but also the healthiest.

National Resource Defense Council
www.nrdc.org

Founded in 1970, this organization is a feisty militant group that, like the Environmental Defense Fund, puts lawyers together with scientists to fight in courtrooms. Their website has a regularly updated section called "Take Action," which lists a wide range of current environmental issues on which they hope people will speak out.

The Nature Conservancy
www.nature.org

Founded in 1951, this organization is one of the older environmental groups. They work a great deal with scientists and pride themselves on their nonconfrontational style, which brings locals and fishermen into the problem-solving process. They have initiated a number of interesting projects with West Coast fisheries, Pacific coral reefs, and endangered species in the Caribbean. They also publish an interesting magazine, *Nature Conservancy*.

Ocean Alliance
www.oceanalliance.org

Founded in 1971, this organization is principally concerned about the impact of pollution on whales. It monitors the impact of oil spills and other pollution by means of a 93-foot sail-powered steel-hulled ship rigged as an oceangoing science laboratory.

Oceana
na.oceana.org

Started in 2001, this organization has generated some suspicion because several of its founders derive their money from oil companies, including the Pew Charitable Trust (Sun Oil), the Marisla Foundation (Getty Oil), and the Rockefeller Brothers Fund (Standard Oil). But keep in mind that these oil companies did their damage several generations ago. In 2002, Oceana merged with American Oceans Campaign, which got its money from actor Ted Danson. Their website has a great deal of information.

The Whaleman Foundation
www.whaleman.org

This is a narrowly focused group that concerns itself only with marine mammals and their habitat, which is, of course, the oceans. If you are primarily interested in whales, porpoises, and dolphins, then you should check them out, as well as their films and other material.

This is a copy of the Seafood Watch pocket guide from July 2010. The Monterey Bay Aquarium updates this guide twice a year, so by the time this book is in bookstores, this particular guide will be out of date. But I have included it as a sample of the kinds of guides that are available from several organizations. Such lists are not infallible but they are a starting point.

MONTEREY BAY AQUARIUM

Seafood WATCH®

YELLOWFIN TUNA

National Sustainable Seafood Guide
July 2010

Learn More

Our recommendations are researched by Monterey Bay Aquarium scientists. For more information about your favorite seafoods, including items not listed here, visit **www.seafoodwatch.org.**

Pocket guides are updated twice yearly. Get current information on your mobile device, on our website or by adding our free app to your iPhone.

MONTEREY BAY
AQUARIUM®

You Can Make A Difference

Support ocean-friendly seafood in three easy steps:

1. Purchase seafood from the green list or, if unavailable, the yellow list. Or look for the Marine Stewardship Council blue eco-label in stores and restaurants.

CERTIFIED SUSTAINABLE SEAFOOD
MSC www.msc.org

2. When you buy seafood, ask where your seafood comes from and whether it was farmed or wild-caught.

3. Tell your friends about Seafood Watch. The more people that ask for ocean-friendly seafood, the better!

Why Do Your Seafood Choices Matter?

Worldwide, the demand for seafood is increasing. Yet many populations of the large fish we enjoy eating are over-fished and, in the U.S., we import over 80% of our seafood to meet the demand. Destructive fishing and fish farming practices only add to the problem.

By purchasing fish caught or farmed using environmentally friendly practices, you're supporting healthy, abundant oceans.

BEST CHOICES

Arctic Char (farmed)
Barramundi (US farmed)
Catfish (US farmed)
Clams (farmed)
Cobia (US farmed)
Cod: Pacific (Alaska longline)
Crab: Dungeness, Stone
Halibut: Pacific
Lobster: Spiny (US)
Mussels (farmed)
Oysters (farmed)
Sablefish/Black Cod (Alaska or BC)
Salmon (Alaska wild)
Scallops (farmed off-bottom)
Shrimp, Pink (OR)
Striped Bass (farmed or wild*)
Tilapia (US farmed)
Trout: Rainbow (farmed)
Tuna: Albacore including canned white tuna (troll/pole, US and BC)
Tuna: Skipjack including canned light tuna (troll/pole)

GOOD ALTERNATIVES

Caviar, Sturgeon (US farmed)
Clams (wild)
Cod: Pacific (US trawled)
Crab: Blue* King (US), Snow
Flounders, Soles (Pacific)
Herring: Atlantic
Lobster: American/Maine
Mahi Mahi/Dolphinfish (US)
Oysters (wild)
Pollock (Alaska wild)
Salmon (WA wild)*
Sablefish/Black Cod (CA, OR and WA)
Scallops: Sea
Shrimp (US, Canada)
Squid
Swai, Basa (farmed)
Swordfish (US)*
Tilapia (Central America, farmed)
Tuna: Bigeye, Yellowfin (troll/pole)
Tuna: Canned white/Albacore (troll/pole except US and BC)

AVOID

Caviar, Sturgeon* (imported wild)
Chilean Seabass/Toothfish*
Cobia (imported farmed)
Cod: Atlantic, imported Pacific
Flounders, Halibut, Soles (Atlantic)
Groupers*
Lobster: Spiny (Brazil)
Mahi Mahi/Dolphinfish (imported)
Marlin: Blue*, Striped*
Monkfish
Orange Roughy*
Salmon (CA, OR* wild)
Salmon (farmed, including Atlantic)*
Sharks*, Skates
Shrimp (imported)
Snapper: Red
Swordfish (imported)*
Tilapia (Asia farmed)
Tuna: Albacore, Bigeye, Yellowfin (longline)*
Tuna: Bluefin*and Tongol
Tuna: Canned (except troll/pole)*

Support Ocean-Friendly Seafood

Best Choices are abundant, well-managed and caught or farmed in environmentally friendly ways.

Good Alternatives are an option, but there are concerns with how they're caught or farmed – or with the health of their habitat due to other human impacts.

Avoid for now as these items are overfished or caught or farmed in ways that harm other marine life or the environment.

Key
BC = British Columbia   CA = California
OR = Oregon   WA = Washington
* Limit consumption due to concerns about mercury or other contaminants.
Visit www.edf.org/seafoodhealth

Contaminant information provided by:
ENVIRONMENTAL DEFENSE FUND

Seafood may appear in more than one column

NINE STEPS TOWARD BUILDING A MOVEMENT

1. Talk a lot about the issues with your friends. Read and see films, exchange ideas.

2. Form a small group. Talk to each other, but also talk to strangers and try to bring them into your group.

3. Give your group a catchy name, like "Student Organized Biodiversity Society" (SOBS).

4. Carry out small, local, doable actions. Circulate literature. Make posters. Inform people. Or try to get one store to stop carrying something you know is endangered.

5. Publicize what you've accomplished. Tell other kids, their parents—even try talking to the media. Talk to everyone about what you are doing, and why.

6. Once your organization seems solid, open a chapter in another school.

7. Then open another chapter in another school.

8. Take on bigger actions.

9. Try to find people to start chapters in other schools and towns. Do something that no one has thought of before!

SEVEN USEFUL TRAITS OF A MOVEMENT ORGANIZER

1. Be studious. Know everything about your subject. Read books, articles, and websites. Be up on the latest developments.

2. Be funny. Have a sense of fun, and a sense of humor. Make your events fun. Let people laugh. You want people to join your movement, and no one wants to be in a movement where everyone is right, but miserable.

3. Be creative. It takes a great deal of imagination to think up actions that will surprise and get attention.

4. Be empathetic. Care about other people's points of view, and their feelings—and don't be embarrassed to show it.

5. Be idealistic. Cynicism may at times seem fashionable, but it does not produce results. While it may seem naïve to think you can change things, every measure of progress in the history of humankind has been made by people who were idealistic enough to believe they could do something.

6. Be respectful. A successful movement is built by people with differing points of view. Treat everyone with kindness and respect—even your opponents. It will disarm those who disagree with your opinion, and inspire those who already agree with you.

7. Be patient. Change is a slow process with many setbacks. If your goals are clear and your determination unshakeable, you can win, in time.

FIVE THINGS YOU CAN DO TO SAVE THE OCEANS AND THE FISH

1. Talk about the issues with your friends, family, and at school.

2. Study up on fisheries, demand information from fish sellers, and get your family to try to buy fish from sustainable fisheries only. Try to identify the best fisheries, and get your family to buy their fish.

3. Write letters to your government representatives expressing your concerns about fish, pollution, global warming, and offshore oil drilling.

4. Never take a ride—not even on public transportation—if you can walk or ride a bicycle instead.

5. Refuse to drink beverages from plastic bottles. Do not use plastic containers to store food. Don't accept plastic bags from stores. Less plastic in the world would be a huge step forward to saving the oceans.

INDEX

ACKNOWLEDGMENTS

I want to thank my agent, Charlotte Sheedy, for bringing this to the right people; my editor, Raquel Jaramillo, for putting it together with so much energy and passion, for caring about the ocean and kids; and Frank Stockton, for the inspiring art. A big thanks to Talia Feiga Kurlansky, my fishing buddy and chief advisor on kids (also my daughter).

Thanks to Frank Lauria for help with the jellyfish recipe.

I would especially like to thank the following biologists for guiding, teaching, and inspiring me: Lisa Balance, Nancy Knowlton, Sarah Mesnick, Daniel Pauly, Michael Sutton, and Edward O. Wilson. If you want an interesting perspective on the world, talk to a biologist.